# THE
# SOULS OF
# YELLOW
# FOLK

# THE
# SOULS OF
# YELLOW
# FOLK

**Essays**

## WESLEY YANG

**W. W. NORTON & COMPANY**
Independent Publishers Since 1923
New York | London

For information about permission to reproduce selections from this book,
write to Permissions, W. W. Norton & Company, Inc.,
500 Fifth Avenue, New York, NY 10110

For information about special discounts for bulk purchases, please contact
W. W. Norton Special Sales at specialsales@wwnorton.com or 800-233-4830


Book design by Michelle McMillian
Production manager: Beth Steidle

ISBN 978-0-393-24174-7

W. W. Norton & Company, Inc., 500 Fifth Avenue, New York, N.Y. 10110
www.wwnorton.com

W. W. Norton & Company Ltd., 15 Carlisle Street, London W1D 3BS

1  2  3  4  5  6  7  8  9  0

*To my wife, Erika Kawalek Yang, who is a model of the strength and integrity I hope to inculcate into our daughter, Vita Yang, with faith that such will be sufficient to confront the world depicted in the pages that follow.*

# CONTENTS

## PART IV

# INTRODUCTION

More than a decade ago, an editor at the literary journal *n+1* asked if I wanted to write about the largest mass murder in American history, which had occurred a few days previously at a college in Virginia. I resented the implication of his request. The implication was that there was something about that episode that would be particularly salient to me. I resented the implication because it was true.

The implication was that we shared something in common, the Virginia Tech killer and I. We were both the children of immigrants from Korea. We were both Asian men in America. Some things that were true then about Asian men in America remain true today: We have the highest educational attainment of any group in America. We have the lowest rate of incarceration. And we have the highest median income in America. So those were a couple of the things I shared in common with the Virginia Tech shooter. We were both part of that fortunate fraction of the American public enrolled in higher education, a part of a busily striving cohort slated to earn a comfortable living in a society that increasingly rewarded the educated and punished the uneducated. We both lived in a society that welcomed diversity, propagandized on its behalf, prided itself on transcending its origins in slavery and genocide. We were both the children of immigrants in a nation of immigrants.

Was that all I had in common with the Virginia Tech killer? The implication I resented was that I would know something, just a little—or maybe a little bit more than a little—about what animated the Virginia Tech killer. I would know this simply because of what we shared in common that extended beyond the high rate of educational attainment, and the low rate of incarceration, that characterized the category of people like ourselves in the aggregate. What we shared in common was that we both had Asian faces.

On the one hand, the Virginia Tech killer was mentally ill. I did not know what it was like to suffer from a clinical condition that culminates in an act of destructive malevolence on a grand scale. On the other hand, the Virginia Tech killer had succumbed to resentment, a much more widely distributed condition, and maybe one that I knew something about. Is that what you're implying? I demanded to know of my editor. I did not receive a reply.

What we were presumed to share in common—and this was the implication that I resented, because it was both true and unspeakable—was the peculiar burden of nonrecognition, of invisibility, that is a condition of being an Asian man in America. You could say, as many have before and since, that we are unused to seeing such faces in the movies and on TV, which was true then, though such a grievance was a poor proxy for the deeper injury that it named: that this face was in our culture a kind of cipher, a void, and all the more so to those of us who had to confront it gazing back at us from a reflected surface.

Was this a real condition or just my own private hallucination? By this I mean something that has in recent years escaped from the obscurity in which it was once shrouded, even as it was always the most salient of all facts, the one most readily on display, the thing that was unspeakable precisely because it need never be spoken: that as the bearer of an Asian face in America, you paid some incremental penalty, never absolute, but always omnipresent, that meant that you were by default unlovable and unloved; that you were presumptively a nobody, a mute and servile figure, distinguishable above all by your total incapacity to threaten anyone; that you were many laudable things that the world might respect and reward, but that you were fundamentally powerless to affect anyone in a way that would make you either loved or feared.

What was the epistemological status of such an extravagant assertion? Could it possibly be true? Could it survive empirical scrutiny? It was a dogmatic statement at once unprovable and unfalsifiable. It was a paranoid statement about the way others regarded you that couldn't possibly be true in any literal sense. It had no real truth value, except that under certain conditions, one felt it with every fiber of one's being to be true. The warm light of day seemed to annul it, reducing this sense to the most lukewarm of all personal conundrums, "Asian-American identity"; the racial grievance least likely to receive, or to deserve, any public recognition, the most readily treated with ironic ridicule. The dark inwardness of nightmare could conjure it back to life: Seung-Hui Cho was the projection of that nightmare, even as he was also a real person who took actual lives.

The bulk of the 10,000-word essay that I wrote was composed in Gmail in one feverish night. My editors and I then proceeded to spend the better part of the next six weeks trying to qualify and contextualize it, to soften its hard edges, and indigestible elements, to bring order and structure and coherence to its digressive dream logic. In the end, we decided to retain the piece's rawness and leave its many loose ends dangling.

It was in many ways an indefensible piece of writing—sprawling, fragmented, bristling with insinuations in the place of argument. It took monstrous liberties, making Cho and his transgressions into a proxy, and a foil. It was about the banality of radical evil, and a strange compound of resentment and entitlement that had accrued in the heart of one young man and caused him to wage war against being itself. It read the manifesto that he circulated to the media in advance of his act as one expression of a fantasy of a mass insurrection that he would summon into being through his act. The manifesto posited the existence of an army of other losers like himself, denied recognition and rendered invisible, who would someday attain class consciousness and leave behind their abjection through violent, coordinated action to subdue the world to their will, or die fighting. And it seems to me today that it bears revisiting primarily as part of the prehistory of our present moment.

In the successive decade, we've grown accustomed to a news cycle punctuated by such acts of motiveless malignity;

typically perpetrated by young men, sometimes inspired by religion, sometimes by race, sometimes by the hatred of women, sometimes by the intersection of each and all. All the rhetorical moves and countermoves in which various partisans frame these eruptions as part of their political agendas are by now routinized, virtually algorithmic. Some blame toxic masculinity, the thwarted entitlement of men; others the ready availability of guns; still others the insufficiency of mental health care. Some invoke the specter of nihilism.

I think about the struggle for recognition. In the successive decade, we've seen the power of the print media and its responsible gatekeepers broken by its digital successor, and the creation of a virtual agon in which the demand for recognition by the hitherto subordinate—by women and minorities—becomes a bid for precedence against those who had always taken it for granted. In the successive decade, the struggle against "racism" and "sexism" shifted rhetorically to a struggle against "whiteness" and "masculinity." This rhetorical shift may have started as the contagious adoption of trendy lingo on social media, but the underlying concept has spread along with the verbal tic: that there is no whiteness independent of domination of nonwhites, and there is no masculinity whose constitutive predicate is not the domination of women. There is therefore no such thing as reforming, accommodating, or coming to terms with either. No one can hope to live free of oppression so long as these categories of being have not been eradicated.

We've seen the emergence of a party of white male resentment which, through coordinated online action seeks to colonize minds and subdue the world to its will. This struggle over the racial and sexual constitution is at once covert, part of the hidden substructure of national politics and our collective life, and obscenely omnipresent, right out there in the open for all to see. My interest has always been in the place where sex and race are both obscenely conspicuous and yet consciously suppressed, largely because of the liminal place that the Asian man occupies in the midst of it: an "honorary white" person who will always be denied the full perquisites of whiteness; an entitled man who will never quite be regarded or treated as a man; a nominal minority whose claim to be a "person of color" deserving of the special regard reserved for victims is taken seriously by no one. In an age characterized by the politics of resentment, the Asian man knows something of the resentment of the embattled white man, besieged on all sides by grievances and demands for reparation, and something of the resentments of the rising social-justice warrior, who feels with every fiber of their being that all that stands in the way of the attainment of their thwarted ambitions is nothing so much as a white man. Tasting of the frustrations of both, he is denied the entitlements of either.

This condition of marginality is both the cause and the effect of his erasure—and perhaps the source of his claim to his centrality, indeed his universality. That lies at the end of a cultural project that has scarcely even begun; at best, we can sketch the contours of what that might look like at some future date that might never arrive.

# THE
# SOULS OF
# YELLOW
# FOLK

# PART I

# 1

## THE FACE OF SEUNG-HUI CHO

**THE FIRST SCHOOL SHOOTER** of the 1990s was an Asian boy who played the violin. I laughed when I heard an account of the rampage from my friend Ethan Gooding, who had survived it. Ethan forgave me my reaction. I think he knew by then that most people, facing up to a real atrocity, as opposed to the hundreds they'd seen on TV, didn't know how to act.

Ethan had left New Providence High School in central New Jersey for the progressive utopia of Simon's Rock College of Bard in Great Barrington, Massachusetts. Simon's Rock was a school for high school juniors and seniors ready for college-level work, a refuge for brilliant misfits, wounded prodigies, and budding homosexuals. Ethan was a pretty bright kid, brighter than me, but mostly he was a budding homosexual. One day in gym class at New Providence, Ethan made a two-handed set shot from half-court using a kickball while dressed in buttercup-yellow short-shorts and earned the nickname "Maurice." This was not a reference to E. M. Forster's frank novel of gay love, but to Maurice Cheeks, the great Philadelphia 76ers point guard. The unintended resonance was savored by those few of us who could discern it. Ethan had a striking pre-Raphaelite pallor set off against flaming red cheeks and lips with the puckered epicene aspect that speaking the French language too young will impart to a decent American mouth. None of this in itself meant, necessarily, that he was going to become gay, but then—well, he was.

Gay-bashing was less of a hate crime back then and more of a patriotic duty, particularly in a race-segregated, heavily Catholic suburb like New Providence. At Youth & Government, the YMCA-sponsored mock legislature attended by suck-ups with Napoleon complexes, the "governor" from our school introduced a bill to "build an island of garbage off of the Jersey Shore" where we could "put all the homosexuals." We all chortled along, none more loudly than the closet cases in our midst. It was the kind of place you wanted to flee so badly that you trained yourself to forget the impulse.

But then there was a place called New York, only a half-hour's drive away. We made our first anxious forays into New York City nightlife, Ethan and I and Jasper Chung, the other Korean kid from my high school (himself a governor of the mock legislature, and also a closet homosexual). We tried to get into the back room of the Limelight, where the real party was happening. "Try to look cute," Ethan told me, brushing my hair with a concerned, appraising look. Then he sucked in his cheeks, which I guess was his way of looking cute, or at least making his face less round. It would be more than a decade and a half before I learned what a smile could do for you (it is one way to hold at bay the world's cruelty), so I made a fish-eyed grimace in emulation of David Gahan of Depeche Mode. They never let us into the back room.

Those were the wild Peter Gatien days, when the place was still bristling with drugs and prostitution, most of which managed to pass us by. But we were assailed by a phalanx of sweaty, shirtless Long Island beefcake. Ethan would, to my frightened astonishment, meet other guys, and go off into a dark corner with them, and leave me to fend for myself, which I was not equipped to do. I'd get dehydrated and wear an anxious scowl. I would attempt some rudimentary sociological and semiotic reading of the scene that swirled all around me. I couldn't relax.

Not that I was myself homosexual. True, my heterosexuality was notional. I wasn't much to look at (skinny, acne-prone, brace-faced, bespectacled, and Asian), and inasmuch as I was ugly, I also had a bad personality. While Ethan was easing himself into same-sex experimentation, I was learning about the torments and transports of misanthropy. "That kid," I remember overhearing one of the baseball players say, "is a misfit." No one ever shoved my head in a locker, the way they did the one amber-tinted Afghani kid, or P. J., the big dumb sweet slow kid, and nobody ever pelted me with rocks, as they did Doug Urbano, who was fat and working-class (his father was a truck driver, and sometimes, when he lectured us about the vital role that truck drivers play in the American economy—they really do, you know—he was jeered). But these judgments stayed with me.

Jasper once told me that I was "essentially unlovable." I've always held that observation close to my heart, turning to it often. It's true of some people—that there's no reason anyone should love or care about them, because they aren't appealing on the outside, and that once you dig into the real person beneath the shell (if, for some obscure if not actively perverse reason, you bother), you find the real inner ugliness. I knew lots of people like that—unloved because unlovable. Toward them I was always cold. Maybe I held them at arm's length to disguise from myself our shared predicament. And so, by trying to disguise something from yourself, you declare it to everyone else—because part of what makes a person unlovable is his inability to love.

One day we were hanging out with Ethan in Jasper's room over winter break. Ethan was telling us all about Simon's Rock, and—this might be an invented memory; it feels real, yet I can't rely on it; the very feeling of reality makes me distrust it—Ethan told me that I reminded him of this weird Asian guy at his school, whom he then proceeded to describe. Ethan, cherubic complexion notwithstanding, could actually be pretty mean. He was proud of his ability to wound with a well-chosen phrase coined in an instant, which is not to say that I didn't aspire to the same facility. It's just that he really had it. In any case, Wayne, my double, was an Asian boy ill at ease in the world and he had a chip on his shoulder. His father had been an officer in the Taiwanese air force, and his mother had been a Suzuki-method violin teacher. For a time, Wayne had been among the best violinists in the world in his age group. He was headed along the familiar track of Asian-American assimilation. By the time he arrived at Simon's Rock, he had other things to prove.

The gay guys liked to tease Wayne and intimate that he might be one of them. It was good-natured ribbing, gentle to the extent that it was not tinged with gay malice; and who could begrudge them their share of malice—a little or a lot—

given the world they were entering? On top of everything else, an incurable illness spread by the kind of sex you were already having or else aching to have was killing off a whole generation of your predecessors. You could get a rise out of Wayne, and he deserved it: here he was at this place where people were finally free to be who they really were, and who he really was turned out to be someone who didn't want other people to be free to be who they were. He had fled Montana only to discover his continuing allegiance to its mores. And who knows, conceivably he was even a bit bi-curious. "How tough are you?" Wayne's friends used to ask him, egging him on. "I'm tough!" he would shout.

By now the story of Wayne Lo has been well told, though he has not become a figure of American legend. (His certified authentic "murderabilia" drawings were fetching just $7.50 on his website at the time his jailers shut it down.) On Monday, December 14, 1992, a package arrived for him in the mail from a North Carolina company called Classic Arms. It contained two hundred rounds of ammunition that Wayne had ordered using his mother's credit card. The school's dean held the package, and, after questioning Wayne about what was inside it (Wayne assured him that it was a Christmas gift), gave it back to him. Liberals! They'll hand over the ammunition that their enemies will use to kill them.

Ethan told his version of the story to Jasper and me over hamburgers at the A&W Restaurant at the Short Hills Mall. Wayne had started hanging out with some other students who wanted to rebel against the orthodoxy of difference at Simon's Rock. They listened to Rush Limbaugh and joked about killing people. They were suspicious of Jews and blacks

and homosexuals and . . . did they make an official exception
for Asians? Wayne wrote a paper proposing a solution to the
AIDS crisis: Kill them all. He lacked the imagination to come
up with the island of garbage disposal. Then, according to
psychiatrists hired by his defense, Wayne was overtaken by a
"somatic hallucination"—not heard, but directly experienced
in his body—of God urging him to punish the sinners of
Simon's Rock.

It was a more innocent time, in a way. The Berlin Wall
had come down. Crime rates were beginning the historic
fall they were to make during the 1990s. American soldiers
were ensconced in the Persian Gulf, having recently kept the
armies of Saddam Hussein from entering the land of the two
holy places. People didn't know about school shooters back
then. They still thought that Asian men were happy to be
(as Ethan liked to call us) the Other White People. Or even,
as many people were suggesting, the New Jews. And for the
most part, Asian people were happy—and are. I mean, maybe
they were nerds, maybe they were faceless drones, but did
anybody know they were angry? What could they be angry
about? They were getting rich with the rest of America—and
reassuring everyone of our openness and our tolerance for
everyone prepared to embrace the American dream.

Lo went around the campus with the Chinese-made SKS
carbine rifle that he bought in a neighboring town. He shot
and killed two people and wounded four others. Had his rampage not ended prematurely when his rifle repeatedly jammed
(cheap Chinese junk), he might have set a record that no one
was going to best. Instead, he called the police and negotiated
his surrender.

————————

**THE PERPETRATOR OF THE** largest mass murder in American history was an Asian boy who wrote poems, short stories, a novel, and plays. I gazed at the sad blank mug of Seung-Hui Cho staring out at the world on CNN.com—the face-forward shot that was all the press had before they received Cho's multimedia manifesto, mailed on the day of the shootings, with its ghastly autoerotic glamour shots (Cho pointing gun at camera; Cho with a hammer; Cho pointing gun at his head). I felt, looking at the photo, a very personal revulsion. Millions of others reviled this person, but my own loathing was more intimate. Those lugubrious eyes, that elongated face behind wire-frame glasses: He looks like me, I thought.

This was another inappropriate reaction. But the photo leapt out at me at a funny time in my life. I had come to New York five years earlier, to create a life for myself there. I had not created a life for myself there. I had wanted to find the emerging writers and thinkers of my generation. I had found the sycophants, careerists, and media parasites who were redefining mediocrity for the twenty-first century. I had wanted to remain true to myself as a writer, and also to succeed; I wanted to be courageous and merciless in defense of the downtrodden, and I wanted to be celebrated for it. This was a naïve and puerile desire and one that could not be realized—at least not by me, not in this world. It could not be done without a facility (and a taste) for ingratiation that I lacked. It could not be done without first occupying a position of strength and privilege that I did not command—because, as Jesus said, to him who hath, more will be given; nor without being enterprising and calculating in a way that I wasn't—because, as Jesus went on to say, to him who hath not, even that which he hath will be taken from him. It seemed to me that every kind of life, and even the extinction of life, was preferable to the one that I was living, which is not to say I had the strength either to change my life, or to end it.

And then to be confronted by that face. Because physiognomy is a powerful thing. It establishes identification and aversion, and all the more so in an age that is officially colorblind. Such impulses operate beneath the gaze of the supervisory intelligence, at a visceral level that may be the most honest part of us. You see a face that looks like yours. You know that there's an existential knowledge you have in common with that face. Both of you know what it's like to have a cultural code superimposed atop your face, and if it's a code that abashes, nullifies, and unmans you, then you confront every visible reflection of that code with a feeling of mingled curiosity and wariness. When I'm out by myself in the city—at the movies or at a restaurant—I'll often see other Asian men out by themselves in the city. We can't even look at each other for the strange vertigo we induce in one another.

Let's talk about legible faces. You know those short, brown-toned South American immigrants that pick your fruit, slaughter your meat, and bus your tables? Would you—a respectable person with a middle-class upbringing—ever consider going on a date with one of them? It's a rude question, because it affects to inquire into what everyone gets to know at the cost of forever leaving it unspoken. But if you were to put your unspoken thoughts into words, they might sound something like this: Not only are these people bus-ing the tables, slaughtering the meat, and picking the fruit; they are the descendants of the people who bused the tables, slaughtered the meat, and picked the fruit of the Aztecs and Incas. The Spanish colonizers slaughtered or mixed their blood with the princes, priests, scholars, artisans, warriors, and beautiful women of the indigenous Americas, leaving untouched a class of Morlocks bred for good-natured servility and thus now tailor-made to the demands of an increasingly feudal postindustrial America. That's, by the way, part of the emotional undertow of the immigration debate, the thing that makes an honest appraisal of the issue impossible, because you can never put anything right without first admitting you're in the wrong.

So: Seung-Hui Cho's face. A perfectly unremarkable Korean face—beady-eyed, brown-toned, a small plump-lipped mouth, eyebrows high off his eyelids, with crooked glasses perched on his nose. It's not an ugly face, exactly; it's not a badly made face. It's just a face that has nothing to do with the desires of women in this country. It's a face belonging to a person who, if he were emailing you, or sending you instant messages, and you were a normal, happy, healthy American girl at an upper second-tier American university—and that's what Cho was doing in the fall of 2005, emailing and writing instant messages to girls—you would consider reporting it to campus security. Which is what they did, the girls who were contacted by Cho.

FIRST, YOU IMAGINE, they tried to dissuade him in the usual way. You try to be polite, but also to suggest that you'd actually prefer that your correspondent, if he could, you know, maybe—oh, I don't know—*Disappear from your life forever? How about that?*—and you had to do this subtly enough not to implicate yourself in anything damaging to your own self-image as a nice person, but then not so subtly that your correspondent would miss the point. When Cho missed the point, the girls had to call the campus police. They did not want him arrested, and they did not press charges. They just had to make clear that while Cho thought he was having one kind of encounter (a potentially romantic one), he was in fact having another kind of encounter (a potentially criminal one), and to show him that the state would intervene on their behalf if he couldn't come to terms with this reality. And so, the police didn't press any charges, but they did have a man-to-man talk with Cho, and conveyed to him the message that it would be better if he cut it out.

Seung-Hui Cho's is the kind of face for which the appropriate response to an expression of longing or need involves armed guards. I am not questioning the choices that these girls made; I am affirming those choices. But I'm talking about the Cho that existed before anyone was killed by him—the one who showed proficiency in beer pong at the one fraternity party his roommates took him to, and who told his roommates he had a girlfriend named Jelly who was a supermodel from outer space; who called one of his roommates to tell him that he had been on vacation with Vladimir Putin; and who emailed Lucinda Roy, director of the Creative Writing program, seeking guidance about how to submit his novel to publishers. "My novel is relatively short," he wrote. "It's sort of like Tom Sawyer, except that it's really silly or pathetic, depending on how you look at it."

Of course, there are a lot of things that Cho might have done to change his social fortunes that he declined to do. Either out of incompetence, stubbornness, or plain old bat-shit craziness, Cho missed many boats that might have ferried him away from his dark fate. For one, he could have dressed a little bit better. He might have tried to do something with his hair. Being a little less bat-shit crazy couldn't have hurt. Above all, he could have cultivated his taste in music. He was "obsessed with downloading music from the Internet," the press reported, putting a sinister cast on something that everyone of a certain age does. But the song he continually played on his laptop, driving his roommates to distraction, wasn't some nihilistic rhapsody of wasted youth. It wasn't Trent Reznor of Nine Inch Nails saying he wanted to fuck you like an animal, and it wasn't the thick lugubrious whine of James Hetfield of Metallica declaring that what he'd felt, and what he'd known, never shone through in what he'd shown.

No, it was the cruddiest, most generic grunge-rock anthem of the nineties, Collective Soul's "Shine." "Shine" came out in 1994, and you only had to hear the first minute to know that whatever was truly unyielding about the music Nirvana spawned by breaking punk into the mainstream was already finished. The song cynically mouths "life-affirming" clichés noxious to the spirit of punk rock, but then these are not, given the situation, without their own pathos. You could picture the Cho who stalked around campus not saying a word to anyone, even when a classmate offered him money to speak, coming home in silence to listen to these lyrics repeat in an infinite loop on his laptop, and even, one day, to write them on his wall:

*Tell me will love be there (love be there)*
*Whoa-oh-oh-oh, heaven let your light shine down.*

**"YOU WERE THE SINGLE BIGGEST DORK** school shooter of all time,"
opined one Internet chat board participant, and it was hard
to disagree. Cho was so disaffected that he couldn't even get
the symbols of disaffection right. In the fall of 2005, when
he made the mistake of instant-messaging girls, Cho was also
attending Nikki Giovanni's large creative writing class. He
would wear reflector glasses with a baseball cap obscuring
his face. Giovanni, who believed that openness was vital to
the goals of the class, stood by his desk at the beginning of
each session to make him take off the disguise. He later began
showing up with a scarf wrapped around his head, "Bedouin-
style," as Giovanni put it. When the attendance sheet was
passed around, he signed his name as a question mark.

The class set Cho off, somehow—maybe because he had
enrolled in the hope that his genius would be recognized, and
it was not recognized. He began snapping pictures of female
classmates with his cell-phone camera from underneath his
desk. Eventually, many of the seventy students enrolled in
the class stopped coming. That's when Giovanni went to
Lucinda Roy and insisted that Cho be barred from her workshop. She refused, in the words of one article about it, to be
"bullied" by Cho.

"He was writing, just weird things," Giovanni told the
*New York Times.* "I don't know if I'm allowed to say what he
was writing about. . . . He was writing poetry, it was terrible,
it was not like poetry, it was intimidating."

Giovanni's personal website has a list of all her honors and awards and another page for all the honorary degrees she has earned—nineteen since 1972—and a brief biography that identifies her as "a world-renowned poet, writer, commentator, activist, and educator," whose "outspokenness, in her writing and in lectures, has brought the eyes of the world upon her." Oprah Winfrey has named her one of her twenty-five living legends. "We are sad today, and we will be sad for quite a while," the sixty-three-year-old eminence told the convocation to mourn Seung-Hui Cho's victims. "We are not moving on, we are embracing our mourning."

It's a perfectly consistent picture: Giovanni the winner of awards, and Giovanni the wise and grandmotherly presence on *Oprah*. But if you knew more about the writing of Nikki Giovanni, you couldn't help but wonder two things. What would the Nikki Giovanni of 2007 have made of a poem published by the Nikki Giovanni of 1968, and what would the Nikki Giovanni of 1968 have made of the Nikki Giovanni of the present? The Nikki Giovanni of 1968 wrote a poem that consisted of a series of variations on the following theme:

*Can a nigger kill a honkie*
*Can a nigger kill the Man*
*Huh? nigger can you*
*kill*
*Do you know how to draw blood*
*Can you poison*
*Can you stab-a-Jew*
*Can you kill huh? nigger*
*Can you kill*

Back then Giovanni was writing about a race war that seemed like it really might break out at home, even as the country was fighting what she saw as an imperialist war in Vietnam. Black militancy was something that many people admired, and many more felt sympathy toward, given the brutal history of enslavement, rape, terrorism, disenfranchisement, lynching, and segregation that blacks had endured in this country. And so you wonder what would have happened if, for instance, Cho's poems (and thoughts) had found a way to connect his pain to his ethnic identity. Would Giovanni have been less intimidated if she could have understood Cho as an aggrieved Asian man, instead of an aggrieved man who happened to be Asian? Or if he were black and wrote the way he did? Or if he were Palestinian and managed to tie his violent grievances to a real political conflict existing in the world? (Can you bomb-a-Jew?) Giovanni knows black rage, and she knows the source of women's bitterness. We all do. We know gay pride. We know, in short, identity politics, which, when it isn't acting as a violent outlet for the narcissism of the age, can serve as its antidote, binding people into imagined collectivities capable of taking action to secure their interests and assert their personhood.

Cho did not think of himself as Asian; he did not think of himself ethnically at all. He was a pimply friendless suburban teenager whom no woman would want to have sex with: that's what he was. And it turned out that in his imagination he was a warrior on behalf of every lonely invisible human being in America. This was his ghastly, insane mistake. This is what we learned from the speech Cho gave in the video he mailed to NBC News. For Cho, the cause to fight for is "the dorky kid that [you] publicly humiliated and spat on," whom you treated like "a filthy street dog" and an "ugly, little, retarded, low-life kid"—not just Cho, not just his solitary narcissistic frenzy, but also that of his "children," his "brothers and sisters"—an imagined community of losers who would leave behind their status as outcasts from the American consensus and attain the dignity of warriors—by killing innocent civilians.

Cho enclosed his speech, too, in the NBC packet, as "writings."

*You had everything you wanted.*
*Your Mercedes wasn't enough,*
*you brats,*
*your golden necklaces weren't enough,*
*you snobs,*
*your trust fund wasn't enough . . .*
    *You have vandalized my heart,*
*raped my soul*
*and torched my conscience.*
*You thought it was one pathetic, void life you were extinguishing.*
    *I die like Jesus Christ,*
*to inspire generations of the weak and defenseless people.*

Cho imagines the one thing that can never exist—the coming to consciousness and the joining in solidarity of the modern class of losers. Though his soft Asian face could only have been a hindrance to him, Cho did not perceive his pain as stemming from being Asian: he did not perceive himself in a world of identity politics, of groups and fragments of groups, of groups oppressing and fighting other groups. Cho's world is a world of individually determined fortunes, of winners and losers in the marketplace of status, cash, and expression. Cho sees a system of social competition that renders some people absolutely immiserated while others grow obscenely rich.

**WHEN I WAS AT RUTGERS,** I knew a guy named Samuel Goldfarb. Samuel was prematurely middle-aged, not just in his dimensions, which were bloated, and not just in his complexion, which was pale but flushed with the exertion of holding himself upright—sweat would dapple the groove between his upper lip and nose—but above all in something he exuded, which was a pheromone of loneliness and hostility. Samuel had gone off to Reed College, and, after a couple of years of feeling alienated in that liberal utopia, he had returned east. Samuel was one of the students at Rutgers who was clearly more intellectually sophisticated than I. He knew more, he had read more, and it showed. He was the kind of nominal left-winger who admired the works of Carl Schmitt before many others had gotten onto that trend, and he knew all about the Frankfurt School, and he was already jaded about the postmodernists when others were still enraptured by the discovery of them. In addition to being the kind of leftist who read a Nazi legal theorist to be contrarian, Samuel was also the kind of aspiring academic so contemptuous of the postmodern academy that he was likely to go into investment banking and make pots of money while jeering at the rest of humanity, because that was so much more punk rock than any other alternative to it. He identified his "lifestyle"—and of course he put that word into derisive quote marks when he used it—as "indie rock," but Samuel's irony had extra bite to it, real cruelty and rancor, that was tonally off-kilter for the indie rock scene, which, as it manifested itself at Rutgers, was taciturn to the point of autism, passive-aggressive, and anti-intellectual, but far too cool and subdued for the exertions of overt cruelty.

You saw a look of sadness and yearning in Samuel's face when he had subsided from one of his misanthropic tirades—there was no limit to the scorn he heaped on the intellectual pretensions of others—and it put you on guard against him. What you sensed about him was that his abiding rage was closely linked to the fact that he was fat and ugly in a uniquely unappealing way, and that this compounded with his unappealing rage made him the sort of person that no woman would ever want to touch. He seemed arrayed in that wild rancor that sexual frustration can bestow on a man, and everything about his persona—his coruscating irony, his unbelievable intellectual snobbery—seemed a way to channel and thus defend himself against this consuming bitterness. He was ugly on the outside, and once you got past that you found the true ugliness on the inside.

And then below that ugliness you found a vulnerable person who desperately needed to be seen and touched and known as a human phenomenon. And above all, you wanted nothing to do with that, because once you touched the source of his loneliness, there would be no end to it, and even if you took it upon yourself to appease this unappeasable need, he would eventually decide to revenge himself against a world that had held him at bay, and there would be no better target for this revenge than you, precisely because you were the person who'd dared to draw the nearest. This is what you felt instantly, without having to put it into words (it's what I felt, anyway, though it might have been pure projection), the moment you met Samuel. For all that he could be amusing to talk to, and for all that he was visibly a nice guy despite all I've just said, you were careful to keep your distance.

Samuel used to complain about declining academic standards. He said that without much work he was acing all of his classes. This was a way of exalting himself slightly while mostly denigrating others, which made it an exemplary statement of his, but it was also a suspect statement, since no one had asked. One day, while I was in the history department's front office, I noticed a plastic crate full of hanging folders. In one of those folders, I found my own academic transcript in its entirety. Then I looked for Samuel's. Like mine, it was riddled with D's and F's. And while what Samuel had said about academic standards and his own aptitude was surely true, it was also true that he had lied—and I suppose I understand why. If your only claim to self-respect was your intellectual superiority, and you had more or less flunked out of Reed College because of the crushing loneliness and depression you encountered once you realized that liberal utopia wasn't going to embrace you as it did the willowy, stylish high school outcasts who surrounded you—and if your grades weren't much better at Rutgers (a pathetic public university, even though you hated Reed more), you might be forced to lie about those grades, because they were the public face of all you had left—your intellectual superiority—and even after all you'd endured, or maybe because of it, your public face still mattered. Unaware that the contrary evidence was there for anyone to check (it should not have been) or that a person inclined to check it existed (I should not have looked), you would assume that you could tell this lie without being caught.

I mentioned this incident to a mutual acquaintance, who proceeded to tell Samuel, who accused me of making up lies about him, and turned me into the great enemy of his life— he was clearly looking for one—which was too bad and a little disconcerting, because, as I explained to him, he and his grades had never meant anything to me. And yet I had only read two transcripts, his and mine, mostly because I suspected, correctly, that he was telling lies. Samuel had been wronged by me, and it would have been right for me to apologize, but I had some hostility of my own, so instead I told him that he was ugly on the outside, but even uglier on the inside, and that he meant nothing to me, and his enmity counted for nothing to me. And this was true. I had recognized him as a person with whom I had some mutual understanding—overlapping interests and, most of all, over-lapping pretensions—but I never wanted him as a friend. The image this whole affair calls up is the scene in *Born on the Fourth of July* in which two paraplegics in wheelchairs start wrestling around in anger, and then tip each other into a ditch by the side of the road, and fall out of their wheelchairs, and roll around on the ground in the dirt, from which they are unable to lift themselves.

I saw Samuel Goldfarb at a coffee shop near Union Square about a year ago. He was chatting up the East European counter girls. You could tell that he was a regular. He had put on a lot of weight and lost more of his hair, and his skin had lost none of its sebaceous excess. He had really become, at thirty-two or thirty-three, the ruined middle-aged man that he already seemed on the cusp of becoming in youth. He seemed like a nice, harmless guy, but then you could still discern loneliness and sexual desperation clinging to him, though it had lost some of its virulence. I was glad to see his resignation. And I knew that he was probably very rich, and I felt weirdly good on his behalf to know that if he had to be lonely, if he had to be one of the millions of sexually null men in America—and for all I knew, he could have studied the Game and become a world-class seducer in the intervening years, though it seemed unlikely ("Hey guys—quick question for you—do you believe in magic spells?"—I couldn't see it)—at least he could be rich.

Lack of money had taught me the value of money. I had learned that when I didn't have it—and by this I mean, really having none of it, as in, like, nothing, which was most of the time—I would become extremely unhappy. And that when I did have it, even a little bit of it, which was rare, my despondency was assuaged, and I became like a dry and dwindling houseplant that would rally and surge up from out of its dolor when watered. I deduced from this pattern that what I needed to do was find an occupation that would pay me a salary—it was amazing to think how long I had gone without one—and then I would have money all the time, and then I would be, if not happy, at least OK. And to come to this realization seemed a little bit like the moment in *1984* when Winston Smith decides that he loves Big Brother, but then even more than that it just felt like growing up and it felt like life. And so I figured that Samuel was fine; and while I was very far from fine, I thought someday I'd catch on to something and I'd eventually be fine too.

And maybe I still will, at that.

**A FRIEND OF MINE** wrote a book about online dating. She talked to hundreds of people about their experiences. Online, you become the person you've always known yourself to be, deep down. Online, you're explicit about the fact that you are paying for a service, and you're explicit about the fact that what you're paying for is to get what you really want, and what you're paying for is the ability to remove that annoying bit of residual romantic nonsense that gets us into annoying situations in life where we have to face up to the fact that we are rational profit maximizers in nothing so much as those intimate areas where we pretend to be otherwise. And so, people on the dating sites disclose what they really want, and also what they really don't want.

This friend talked to one man from Maryland who put up his profile on Match.com one night a few years back. This man had good reason to think he would do well on the site. He made more than $150,000 a year; he was white; he was over six feet tall. The next morning, he woke up and checked his account. Over the course of the previous night, he had gotten many responses. How many responses had he gotten? How well could he expect to do, being a man able to check off, without lying, boxes that certified that he made more than $150,000 a year, that he was six feet four inches tall, and that he was white? How well do you think he was going to do on that site where people disclosed what they really wanted out of life and also what they really didn't want?

He had gotten six thousand responses in one night. The fact was that if there was something intriguing or beautiful about that man—and there's something beautiful about us all, if you look deeply enough—someone was going to take the trouble to find it out, and they'd love him for that thing, not because he was six feet four inches tall, and not because he made more than $150,000 a year. You'd find out about his love of truth and poetry, to the extent that it existed, or at least his ability to make you laugh, or his own ability to laugh at things that made you laugh too—things on TV. You could watch TV together. Because the thing you wanted to do was to find true love and have that true love coincide with every-thing else that you wanted from life, so that you could have all the benefits of one kind of ease, and all the moral credit that others had to win by forgoing that kind of ease (but you could have it all, so why not?), and so you were going to put yourself in a position to do that. And you weren't going to answer the ads of anyone with beady lugubrious eyes in a forlorn, brown-tinted face, and if that person wrote you a message, you weren't going to write him back, and you'd probably even, if it seemed like it was necessary, block all further emails from that person. And you'd be right to do that. You'd be behaving in the way that any rational person in your situation would behave. We all agree that the rational thing to do is to shut every trace of that person's existence out of your view. The question, though, is—what if it's not you shutting out the losers? What if you're the loser whom everyone is shutting out? Of course, every loser is shutting out an even more wretched loser. But what if, as far as you know, you're the lowest person at the low end of this hierarchy? What is your rational move then?

You wake to find yourself one of the disadvantaged of the fully liberated sexual marketplace. If you are a woman, maybe you notice that men have a habit of using and discarding you, pleading their own inconstancy and premature emotional debauchery as a sop to your wounded feelings. If you are a man, maybe you notice that the women who have been used and discarded by other, more highly valued men are happy to restore (for a while) their own broken self-esteem by stepping on you while you are prone, and reminding you that even a society of outcasts has its hierarchies. Indeed, these hierarchies are policed all the more ruthlessly the closer to the bottom you go.

For these people, we have nothing but options. Therapy, selective serotonin reuptake inhibitors, alcoholism, drug addiction, pornography, training in mixed martial arts, mail-order brides from former Soviet republics, sex tours in Southeast Asia, prostitution, video-game consoles, protein shakes and weightlifting regimens, New Age medicine, obsession with pets or home furnishings, the recovery movement—all of which are modes of survival as opposed to forms of life. Each of these options compensates for a thing, love, that no person can flourish without, and each, in a different way, offers an endlessly deferred resolution to a conundrum that is effectively irresolvable. You could even say that our culture feeds off the plight of the poor in spirit in order to create new dependencies. You might even dare to say that an undernourished human soul—desperate and flailing, prone to seeking voluntary slavery in the midst of freedom and prosperity—is so conducive to the creation of new markets that it is itself the indispensable product of our culture and our time, at once its precondition and its goal.

**THERE'S A FAMILIAR NARRATIVE** we all know about high school losers. It's the narrative of smart sitcoms and even edgy indie films. The high school loser grows up, fills out, goes to Brown or RISD, and becomes the ideal guy for every smart, sensitive, quirky-but-cute girl with glasses (who is, in turn, the female version of the loser made good). The traits that hindered him (or her) in one phase of life turn out to be a blessing in another, more enlightened phase, or else get cast aside. For many people, this is an accurate description of their experience—it is the experience of the writers and producers of these stories.

In the indie film version of Seung-Hui Cho's life, the escort Cho hired a few weeks before his massacre wouldn't have danced for him for fifteen minutes in a motel room and then shoved him away when he tried to touch her. Not every one of the girls he tried to talk to would have recoiled in horror from him. Something would have happened in that film to remind him, and us, of his incipient humanity—that horribly menaced and misshapen thing. He would have found a good-hearted person who had perhaps been touched in some way by the same hysteria—and don't we all know something about it?—that had consumed Cho's soul. And this good-hearted girl or boy would have known how to forgive Cho for what he couldn't forgive himself—the unbearable, all-consuming shame of being ugly, weak, sick, poor, clumsy, and ungifted.

We know that Cho had dreamt of this indie film ending. He had been dreaming of it for a long time. In the spring semester of 2006, he wrote a story about a boy estranged from his classmates: "Everyone is smiling and laughing as if they're in heaven-on-earth, something magical and enchanting about all the people's intrinsic nature that Bud will never experience." But eventually the boy meets a "Gothic Girl," to whom he breaks down and confesses, "I'm nothing. I'm a loser. I can't do anything. I was going to kill every god damn person in this damn school, swear to god I was, but I . . . couldn't. I just couldn't."

Cho's short story about the Gothic Girl should have ended, but did not, with this declaration. Instead, he and the girl steal a car and drive to her house, where she retrieves "a .8 caliber automatic rifle and a M16 machine gun," and the story concludes when she tells the narrator, "You and me. We can fight to claim our deserving throne."

In real life, there was *no* Gothic Girl, no me to Cho's *you*, no other willing actors—whether sympathetic, heroic, or equally violently deranged—to populate the self-made movie of his life.

Having failed to make it as a novelist—he really did send a book proposal to a New York publisher—Cho decided to make a film. This was a familiar trajectory, with a twist. He was going to collaborate with all the major television networks on it. In the days before his date with a self-appointed destiny, Cho was spotted working out in the college gym. He wanted his scrawny arms and chest to appear more credibly menacing than they were. How many of those men working their arms to the point of exhaustion were driven by the vain notion that they could improve their sexual prospects in the process? Cho had no such illusions. He was preparing a spectacle for the world to witness on TV, and he needed to look the part.

*n+1, 2008*

## 2

# PAPER TIGERS

SOMETIMES I'LL GLIMPSE MY REFLECTION in a window and feel astonished by what I see. Jet-black hair. Slanted eyes. A pancake-flat surface of yellow-and-green-toned skin. An expression that is nearly reptilian in its impassivity. I've contrived to think of this face as the equal in beauty to any other. But what I feel in these moments is its strangeness to me. It's my face. I can't disclaim it. But what does it have to do with me?

Millions of Americans must feel estranged from their own faces. But every self-estranged individual is estranged in his own way. I, for instance, am the child of Korean immigrants, but I do not speak my parents' native tongue. I have never called my elders by the proper honorific, "big brother" or "big sister." I have never dated a Korean woman. I don't have a Korean friend. Though I am an immigrant, I have never wanted to strive like one.

You could say that I am, in the gently derisive parlance of Asian-Americans, a banana or a Twinkie (yellow on the outside, white on the inside). But while I don't believe our roots necessarily define us, I do believe there are racially inflected assumptions wired into our neural circuitry that we use to sort through the sea of faces we confront. And although I am in most respects devoid of Asian characteristics, I do have an Asian face.

Here is what I sometimes suspect my face signifies to other Americans: an invisible person, barely distinguishable from a mass of faces that resemble it. A conspicuous person standing apart from the crowd and yet devoid of any individuality. An icon of so much that the culture pretends to honor but that it in fact patronizes and exploits. Not just people "who are good at math" and play the violin, but a mass of stifled, repressed, abused, conformist quasi-robots who simply do not matter, socially or culturally.

I've always been of two minds about this sequence of stereotypes. On the one hand, it offends me greatly that anyone would think to apply them to me, or to anyone else, simply on the basis of facial characteristics. On the other hand, it also seems to me that there are a lot of Asian people to whom they apply.

Let me summarize my feelings toward Asian values: Fuck filial piety. Fuck grade-grubbing. Fuck Ivy League mania. Fuck deference to authority. Fuck humility and hard work. Fuck harmonious relations. Fuck sacrificing for the future. Fuck earnest, striving middle-class servility.

I understand the reasons Asian parents have raised a generation of children this way. Doctor, lawyer, accountant, engineer: These are good jobs open to whoever works hard enough. What could be wrong with that pursuit? Asians graduate from college at a rate higher than any other ethnic group in America, including whites. They earn a higher median family income than any other ethnic group in America, including whites. This is a stage in a triumphal narrative, and it is a narrative that is much shorter than many remember. Two-thirds of the roughly 14 million Asian-Americans are foreign-born. There were fewer than 39,000 people of Korean descent living in America in 1970, when my elder brother was born. There are around 1 million today.

Asian-American success is typically taken to ratify the American Dream and to prove that minorities can make it in this country without handouts. Still, an undercurrent of racial panic always accompanies the consideration of Asians, and all the more so as China becomes the destination for our industrial base and the banker controlling our burgeoning debt. But if the armies of Chinese factory workers who make our fast fashion and iPads terrify us, and if the collective mass of high-achieving Asian-American students arouse an anxiety about the laxity of American parenting, what of the Asian-American who obeyed everything his parents told him? Does this person really scare anyone?

Earlier this year, the publication of Amy Chua's *Battle Hymn of the Tiger Mother* incited a collective airing out of many varieties of race-based hysteria. But absent from the millions of words written in response to the book was any serious consideration of whether Asian-Americans were in fact taking over this country. If it is true that they are collectively dominating in elite high schools and universities, is it also true that Asian-Americans are dominating in the real world? My strong suspicion was that this was not so, and that the reasons would not be hard to find. If we are a collective juggernaut that inspires such awe and fear, why does it seem that so many Asians are so readily perceived to be, as I myself have felt most of my life, the products of a timid culture, easily pushed around by more assertive people, and thus basically invisible?

A few months ago, I received an email from a young man named Jefferson Mao, who after attending Stuyvesant High School in New York City had recently graduated from the University of Chicago. He wanted my advice about "being an Asian writer." This is how he described himself: "I got good grades and I love literature and I want to be a writer and an intellectual; at the same time, I'm the first person in my family to go to college, my parents don't speak English very well, and we don't own the apartment in Flushing that we live in. I mean, I'm proud of my parents and my neighborhood and what I perceive to be my artistic potential or whatever, but sometimes I feel like I'm jumping the gun a generation or two too early."

One bright, cold Sunday afternoon, I ride the 7 train to its last stop in Flushing, where the storefront signs are all written in Chinese and the sidewalks are a slow-moving river of impassive faces. Mao is waiting for me at the entrance of the Main Street subway station, and together we walk to a nearby Vietnamese restaurant.

Mao has a round face, with eyes behind rectangular wire-frame glasses. Since graduating, he has been living with his parents, who emigrated from China when Mao was eight years old. His mother is a manicurist; his father is a physical therapist's aide. Lately, Mao has been making the familiar hour-and-a-half ride from Flushing to downtown Manhattan to tutor a white Stuyvesant freshman who lives in Tribeca. And what he feels, sometimes, in the presence of that amiable young man is a pang of regret. Now he understands better what he ought to have done back when he was a Stuyvesant freshman: "Worked half as hard and been twenty times more successful."

Entrance to Stuyvesant, one of the most competitive public high schools in the country, is determined solely by performance on a test: The top 3.7 percent of all New York City students who take the Specialized High Schools Admissions Test hoping to go to Stuyvesant are accepted. There are no set-asides for the underprivileged or, conversely, for alumni or other privileged groups. There is no formula to encourage "diversity" or any nebulous concept of "well-roundedness" or "character." Here we have something like pure meritocracy. This is what it looks like: Asian-Americans, who make up 12.6 percent of New York City, make up 72 percent of the high school.

This year, 569 Asian-Americans scored high enough to earn a slot at Stuyvesant, along with 179 whites, 13 Hispanics, and 12 blacks. Such dramatic overrepresentation, and what it may be read to imply about the intelligence of different groups of New Yorkers, has a way of making people uneasy. But intrinsic intelligence, of course, is precisely what Asians don't believe in. They believe—and have proved—that the constant practice of test-taking will improve the scores of whoever commits to it. All throughout Flushing, as well as in Bayside, one can find "cram schools," or storefront academies, that drill students in test preparation after school, on weekends, and during summer break. "Learning math is not about learning math," an instructor at one called Ivy Prep was quoted in the *New York Times* as saying. "It's about weightlifting. You are pumping the iron of math." Mao puts it more specifically: "You learn quite simply to nail any standardized test you take."

And so there is an additional concern accompanying the rise of the Tiger Children, one focused more on the narrowness of the educational experience a non-Asian child might receive in the company of fanatically preprofessional Asian students. Jenny Tsai, a student who was elected president of her class at the equally competitive New York public school Hunter College High School, remembers frequently hearing that "the school was becoming too Asian, that they would be the downfall of our school." A couple of years ago, she revisited this issue in her senior thesis at Harvard, where she interviewed graduates of elite public schools and found that the white students regarded the Asians students with wariness. (She quotes a music teacher at Stuyvesant describing the dominance of Asians: "They were mediocre kids, but they got in because they were coached.") In 2005, the *Wall Street Journal* reported on "white flight" from a high school in Cupertino, California, that began soon after the children of Asian software engineers had made the place so brutally competitive that a B average could place you in the bottom third of the class.

Colleges have a way of correcting for this imbalance: The Princeton sociologist Thomas Espenshade has calculated that an Asian applicant must, in practice, score 140 points higher on the SAT than a comparable white applicant to have the same chance of admission. This is obviously unfair to the many qualified Asian individuals who are punished for the success of others with similar faces. Upper-middle-class white kids, after all, have their own elite private schools, and their own private tutors, far more expensive than the cram schools, to help them game the education system.

You could frame it, as some aggrieved Asian-Americans do, as a simple issue of equality and press for race-blind quantitative admissions standards. In 2006, a decade after California passed a voter initiative outlawing any racial engineering at the public universities, Asians composed 46 percent of UC-Berkeley's entering class; one could imagine a similar demographic reshuffling in the Ivy League, where Asian-Americans currently make up about 17 percent of undergraduates. But the Ivies, as we all know, have their own private institutional interests at stake in their admissions choices, including some that are arguably defensible. Who can seriously claim that a Harvard University that was 72 percent Asian would deliver the same grooming for elite status its students had gone there to receive?

Somewhere near the middle of his time at Stuyvesant, a vague sense of discontent started to emerge within Mao. He had always felt himself a part of a mob of "nameless, faceless Asian kids," who were "like a part of the décor of the place." He had been content to keep his head down and work toward the goal shared by everyone at Stuyvesant: Harvard. But around the beginning of his senior year, he began to wonder whether this march toward academic success was the only, or best, path.

"You can't help but feel like there must be another way," he explains over a bowl of phô. "It's like, we're being pitted against each other while there are kids out there in the Midwest who can do way less work and be in a garage band or something—and if they're decently intelligent and work decently hard in school . . ."

Mao began to study the racially inflected social hierarchies at Stuyvesant, where, in a survey undertaken by the student newspaper this year, slightly more than half of the respondents reported that their friends came from within their own ethnic group. His attention focused on the mostly white (and Manhattan-dwelling) group whose members seemed able to manage the crushing workload while still remaining socially active. "The general gist of most high-school movies is that the pretty cheerleader gets with the big dumb jock, and the nerd is left to bide his time in loneliness. But at some point in the future," he says, "the nerd is going to rule the world, and the dumb jock is going to work in a carwash.

"At Stuy, it's completely different: If you looked at the pinnacle, the girls and the guys are not only good-looking and socially affable, they also get the best grades and star in the school plays and win election to student government. It all converges at the top. It's like training for high society. It was jarring for us Chinese kids. You got the sense that you had to study hard, but it wasn't enough."

Mao was becoming clued in to the fact that there was another hierarchy behind the official one that explained why others were getting what he never had—"a high-school sweetheart" figured prominently on this list—and that this mysterious hierarchy was going to determine what happened to him in life. "You realize there are things you really don't understand about courtship or just acting in a certain way.

Things that somehow come naturally to people who go to school in the suburbs and have parents who are culturally assimilated." I pressed him for specifics, and he mentioned that he had visited his white girlfriend's parents' house the past Christmas, where the family had "sat around cooking together and playing Scrabble." This ordinary vision of suburban-American domesticity lingered with Mao: Here, at last, was the setting in which all that implicit knowledge "about social norms and propriety" had been transmitted. There was no cram school that taught these lessons.

Before having heard from Mao, I had considered myself at worst lightly singed by the last embers of Asian alienation. Indeed, given all the incredibly hip Asian artists and fashion designers and so forth you can find in New York, it seemed that this feeling was destined to die out altogether. And yet here it was in a New Yorker more than a dozen years my junior. While it may be true that sections of the Asian-American world are devoid of alienation, there are large swaths where it is as alive as it has ever been.

A few weeks after we meet, Mao puts me in touch with Daniel Chu, his close friend from Stuyvesant. Chu graduated from Williams College last year, having won a creative-writing award for his poetry. He had spent a portion of the $18,000 prize on a trip to China, but now he is back living with his parents in Brooklyn Chinatown.

Chu remembers that during his first semester at Williams, his junior adviser would periodically take him aside. Was he feeling all right? Was something the matter? "I was acclimating myself to the place," he says. "I wasn't totally happy, but I wasn't depressed." But then his new white friends made similar remarks. "They would say, 'Dan, it's kind of hard, sometimes, to tell what you're thinking.'"

Chu has a pleasant face, but it would not be wrong to characterize his demeanor as reserved. He speaks in a quiet, unemphatic voice. He doesn't move his features much. He attributes these traits to the atmosphere in his household. "When you grow up in a Chinese home," he says, "you don't talk. You shut up and listen to what your parents tell you to do."

At Stuyvesant, he had hung out in an exclusively Asian world in which friends were determined by which subway lines you traveled. But when he arrived at Williams, Chu slowly became aware of something strange: The white people in the New England wilderness walked around smiling at each other. "When you're in a place like that, everyone is friendly."

He made a point to start smiling more. "It was something that I had to actively practice," he says. "Like, when you have a transaction at a business, you hand over the money—and then you smile." He says that he's made some progress but that there's still plenty of work that remains. "I'm trying to undo eighteen years of a Chinese upbringing. Four years at Williams helps, but only so much." He is conscious of how his father, an IT manager, is treated at work. "He's the best programmer at his office," he says, "but because he doesn't speak English well, he is always passed over."

Though Chu is not merely fluent in English but is officially the most distinguished poet of his class at Williams, he still worries that other aspects of his demeanor might attract the same kind of treatment his father received. "I'm really glad we're having this conversation," he says at one point—it is helpful to be remembering these lessons in self-presentation just as he prepares for job interviews.

"I guess what I would like is to become so good at something that my social deficiencies no longer matter," he tells me. Chu is a bright, diligent, impeccably credentialed young man born in the United States. He is optimistic about his ability to earn respect in the world. But he doubts he will ever feel the same comfort in his skin that he glimpsed in the people he met at Williams. That kind of comfort, he says—"I think it's generations away."

WHILE HE WAS STILL an electrical-engineering student at Berkeley in the nineties, James Hong visited the IBM campus for a series of interviews. An older Asian researcher looked over Hong's résumé and asked him some standard questions. Then he got up without saying a word and closed the door to his office.

"Listen," he told Hong, "I'm going to be honest with you. My generation came to this country because we wanted better for you kids. We did the best we could, leaving our homes and going to graduate school not speaking much English. If you take this job, you are just going to hit the same ceiling we did. They just see me as an Asian Ph.D., never management potential. You are going to get a job offer, but don't take it. Your generation has to go farther than we did, otherwise we did everything for nothing."

The researcher was talking about what some refer to as the "Bamboo Ceiling"—an invisible barrier that maintains a pyramidal racial structure throughout corporate America, with lots of Asians at junior levels, quite a few in middle management, and virtually none in the higher reaches of leadership.

The failure of Asian-Americans to become leaders in the white-collar workplace does not qualify as one of the burning social issues of our time. But it is a part of the bitter under-current of Asian-American life that so many Asian graduates of elite universities find that meritocracy as they have under-stood it comes to an abrupt end after graduation. If between 15 and 20 percent of every Ivy League class is Asian, and if the Ivy Leagues are incubators for the country's leaders, it would stand to reason that Asians would make up some cor-responding portion of the leadership class.

And yet the numbers tell a different story. According to a recent study, Asian-Americans represent roughly 5 per-cent of the population but only 0.3 percent of corporate offi-cers, less than 1 percent of corporate board members, and around 2 percent of college presidents. There are nine Asian-American CEOs in the Fortune 500. In specific fields where Asian-Americans are heavily represented, there is a similar asymmetry. A third of all software engineers in Silicon Val-ley are Asian, and yet they make up only 6 percent of board members and about 10 percent of corporate officers of the Bay Area's twenty-five largest companies. At the National Insti-tutes of Health, where 21.5 percent of tenure-track scientists are Asians, only 4.7 percent of the lab or branch directors are, according to a study conducted in 2005. One succinct evoca-tion of the situation appeared in the comments section of a website called Yellowworld: "If you're East Asian, you need to attend a top-tier university to land a good high-paying gig. Even if you land that good high-paying gig, the white guy with the pedigree from a mediocre state university will somehow move ahead of you in the ranks simply because he's white."

Jennifer W. Allyn, a managing director for diversity at PricewaterhouseCoopers, works to ensure that "all of the groups feel welcomed and supported and able to thrive and to go as far as their talents will take them." I posed to her the following definition of parity in the corporate workforce: If the current crop of associates is 17 percent Asian, then in fourteen years, when they have all been up for partner review, 17 percent of those who are offered partner will be Asian. Allyn conceded that PricewaterhouseCoopers was not close to reaching that benchmark anytime soon—and that "nobody else is either."

Part of the insidious nature of the Bamboo Ceiling is that it does not seem to be caused by overt racism. A survey of Asian-Pacific-American employees of Fortune 500 companies found that 80 percent reported they were judged not as Asians but as individuals. But only 51 percent reported the existence of Asians in key positions, and only 55 percent agreed that their firms were fully capitalizing on the talents and perspectives of Asians.

More likely, the discrepancy in these numbers is a matter of unconscious bias. Nobody would affirm the proposition that tall men are intrinsically better leaders, for instance. And yet while only 15 percent of the male population is at least six feet tall, 58 percent of all corporate CEOs are. Similarly, nobody would say that Asian people are unfit to be leaders.

But subjects in a recently published psychological experiment consistently rated hypothetical employees with Caucasian-sounding names higher in leadership potential than identical ones with Asian names.

Maybe it is simply the case that a traditionally Asian upbringing is the problem. As Allyn points out, in order to be a leader, you must have followers. Associates at PricewaterhouseCoopers are initially judged on how well they do the work they are assigned. "You have to be a doer," as she puts it. They are expected to distinguish themselves with their diligence, at which point they become "super-doers." But being a leader requires different skill sets. "The traits that got you to where you are won't necessarily take you to the next level," says the diversity consultant Jane Hyun, who wrote a book called *Breaking the Bamboo Ceiling.* To become a leader requires taking personal initiative and thinking about how an organization can work differently. It also requires networking, self-promotion, and self-assertion. It's racist to think that any given Asian individual is unlikely to be creative or risk-taking. It's simple cultural observation to say that a group whose education has historically focused on rote memorization and "pumping the iron of math" is, on aggregate, unlikely to yield many people inclined to challenge authority or break with inherited ways of doing things.

Sach Takayasu had been one of the fastest-rising members of her cohort in the marketing department at IBM in New York. But about seven years ago, she felt her progress begin to slow. "I had gotten to the point where I was overdelivering, working really long hours, and where doing more of the same wasn't getting me anywhere," she says. It was around this time that she attended a seminar being offered by an organization called Leadership Education for Asian Pacifics.

LEAP has parsed the complicated social dynamics responsible for the dearth of Asian-American leaders and has designed training programs that flatter Asian people even as it teaches them to change their behavior to suit white-American expectations. Asians who enter a LEAP program are constantly assured that they will be able to "keep your values, while acquiring new skills," along the way to becoming "culturally competent leaders."

In a presentation to 1,500 Asian-American employees of Microsoft, LEAP president and CEO J. D. Hokoyama laid out his grand synthesis of the Asian predicament in the workplace. "Sometimes people have perceptions about us and our communities which may or may not be true," Hokoyama told the audience. "But they put those perceptions onto us, and then they do something that can be very devastating: They make decisions about us not based on the truth but based on those perceptions." Hokoyama argued that it was not sufficient to rail at these unjust perceptions. In the end, Asian people themselves would have to assume responsibility for unmaking them. This was both a practical matter, he argued, and, in its own way, fair.

Aspiring Asian leaders had to become aware of "the relationship between values, behaviors, and perceptions." He offered the example of Asians who don't speak up at meetings. "So let's say I go to meetings with you and I notice you never say anything. And I ask myself, 'Hmm, I wonder why you're not saying anything. Maybe it's because you don't know what we're talking about. That would be a good reason for not saying anything. Or maybe it's because you're not even interested in the subject matter. Or maybe you think the conversation is beneath you.' So here I'm thinking, because you never say anything at meetings, that you're either dumb, you don't care, or you're arrogant. When maybe it's because you were taught when you were growing up that when the boss is talking, what are you supposed to be doing? Listening.''

Takayasu took the weeklong course in 2006. One of the first exercises she encountered involved the group instructor asking for a list of some qualities that they identify with Asians. The students responded: upholding family honor, filial piety, self-restraint. Then the instructor solicited a list of the qualities the members identify with leadership, and invited the students to notice how little overlap there is between the two lists.

At first, Takayasu didn't relate to the others in attendance, who were listing typical Asian values their parents had taught them. "They were all saying things like 'Study hard,' 'Become a doctor or lawyer,' blah, blah, blah. That's not how my parents were. They would worry if they saw me working too hard." Takayasu had spent her childhood shuttling between New York and Tokyo. Her father was an executive at Mitsubishi; her mother was a concert pianist. She was highly assimilated into American culture, fluent in English, poised and confident. "But the more we got into it, as we moved away from the obvious things to the deeper, more fundamental values, I began to see that my upbringing had been very Asian after all. My parents would say, 'Don't create problems. Don't trouble other people.' How Asian is that? It helped to explain why I don't reach out to other people for help." It occurred to Takayasu that she was a little bit "heads down" after all. She was willing to take on difficult assignments without seeking credit for herself. She was reluctant to "toot her own horn."

Takayasu has put her new self-awareness to work at IBM, and she now exhibits a newfound ability for horn-tooting. "The things I could write on my résumé as my team's accomplishments: They're really impressive," she says.

The law professor and writer Tim Wu grew up in Canada with a white mother and a Taiwanese father, which allows him an interesting perspective on how whites and Asians perceive each other. After graduating from law school, he took a series of clerkships, and he remembers the subtle ways in which hierarchies were developed among the other young lawyers. "There is this automatic assumption in any legal environment that Asians will have a particular talent for bitter labor," he says, and then goes on to define the word "coolie," a Chinese term for "bitter labor." "There was this weird self-selection where the Asians would migrate toward the most brutal part of the labor."

By contrast, the white lawyers he encountered had a knack for portraying themselves as above all that. "White people have this instinct that is really important: to give off the impression that they're only going to do the really important work. You're a quarterback. It's a kind of arrogance that Asians are trained not to have. Someone told me not long after I moved to New York that in order to succeed, you have to understand which rules you're supposed to break. If you break the wrong rules, you're finished. And so the easiest thing to do is follow all the rules. But then you consign yourself to a lower status. The real trick is understanding what rules are not meant for you."

This idea of a kind of rule-governed rule-breaking— where the rule book was unwritten but passed along in an innate cultural sense—is perhaps the best explanation I have heard of how the Bamboo Ceiling functions in practice. LEAP appears to be very good at helping Asian workers who are already culturally competent become more self-aware of how their culture and appearance impose barriers to advancement. But I am not sure that a LEAP course is going to be enough to get Jefferson Mao or Daniel Chu the respect and success they crave. The issue is more fundamental, the social dynamics at work more deeply embedded, and the remedial work required may be at a more basic level of comportment.

WHAT IF YOU MISSED OUT on the lessons in masculinity taught in the gyms and locker rooms of America's high schools? What if life has failed to make you a socially dominant alpha male who runs the American boardroom and prevails in the American bedroom? What if no one ever taught you how to greet white people and make them comfortable? What if, despite these deficiencies, you no longer possess an immigrant's dutiful forbearance for a secondary position in the American narrative and want to be a player in the scrimmage of American appetite right now, in the present?

How do you undo eighteen years of a Chinese upbringing?

This is the implicit question that J. T. Tran has posed to a roomful of Yale undergraduates at a master's tea at Silliman College. His answer is typically Asian: practice. Tran is a pickup artist who goes by the handle Asian Playboy. He travels the globe running "boot camps," mostly for Asian male students, in the art of attraction. Today, he has been invited to Yale by the Asian-American Students Alliance.

"Creepy can be fixed," Tran explains to the standing-room-only crowd. "Many guys just don't realize how to project themselves." These are the people whom Tran spends his days with, a new batch in a new city every week: nice guys, intelligent guys, motivated guys, who never figured out how to be successful with women. Their mothers had kept them at home to study rather than let them date or socialize. Now Tran's company, ABCs of Attraction, offers a remedial education that consists of three four-hour seminars, followed by a supervised night out "in the field," in which J. T., his assistant Gareth Jones, and a tall blond wing-girl named Sarah force them to approach women. Tuition costs $1,450.

"One of the big things I see with Asian students is what I call the Asian poker face—the lack of range when it comes to facial expressions," Tran says. "How many times has this happened to you?" he asks the crowd. "You'll be out at a party with your white friends, and they will be like—'Dude, are you angry?'" Laughter fills the room. Part of it is psychological, he explains. He recalls one Korean-American student he was teaching. The student was a very dedicated schoolteacher who cared a lot about his students. But none of this was visible. "Sarah was trying to help him, and she was like, 'C'mon, smile, smile,' and he was like . . ." And here Tran mimes the unbearable tension of a face trying to contort itself into a simulacrum of mirth. "He was so completely unpracticed at smiling that he literally could not do it." Eventually, though, the student fought through it, "and when he finally got to smiling he was, like, really cool."

Tran continues to lay out a story of Asian-American male distress that must be relevant to the lives of at least some of those who have packed Master Krauss's living room. The story he tells is one of Asian-American disadvantage in the sexual marketplace, a disadvantage that he has devoted his life to overturning. Yes, it is about picking up women. Yes, it is about picking up white women. Yes, it is about attracting those women whose hair is the color of the midday sun and eyes are the color of the ocean, and it is about having sex with them. He is not going to apologize for the images of blond women plastered all over his website. This is what he prefers, what he stands for, and what he is selling: the courage to pursue anyone you want, and the skills to make the person you desire desire you back. White guys do what they want; he is going to do the same.

But it is about much more than this, too. It is about altering the perceptions of Asian men—perceptions that are rooted in the way they behave, which are in turn rooted in the way they were raised—through a course of behavior modification intended to teach them how to be the socially dominant figures that they are not perceived to be. It is a program of, as he puts it to me later, "social change through pickup."

Tran offers his own story as an exemplary Asian underdog. Short, not good-looking, socially inept, sexually null. "If I got a B, I would be whipped," he remembers of his childhood. After college, he worked as an aerospace engineer at Boeing and Raytheon, but internal politics disfavored him. Five years into his career, his entire white cohort had been promoted above him. "I knew I needed to learn about social dynamics, because just working hard wasn't cutting it."

His efforts at dating were likewise "a miserable failure." It was then that he turned to "the seduction community," a group of men on Internet message boards like alt.seduction .fast.com. It began as a "support group for losers" and later turned into a program of self-improvement. Was charisma something you could teach? Could confidence be reduced to a formula? Was it merely something that you either possessed or did not possess, as a function of the experiences you had been through in life, or did it emerge from specific forms of behavior? The members of the group turned their computer-science and engineering brains to the question. They wrote long accounts of their dates and subjected them to collective scrutiny. They searched for patterns in the raw material and filtered these experiences through social-psychological research. They eventually built a model.

This past Valentine's Day, during a weekend boot camp in New York City sponsored by the ABCs of Attraction, the model is being played out. Tran and Jones are teaching their students how an alpha male stands (shoulders thrown back, neck fully extended, legs planted slightly wider than the shoulders). "This is going to feel very strange to you if you're used to slouching, but this is actually right," Jones says. They explain how an alpha male walks (no shuffling; pick your feet up entirely off the ground; a slight sway in the shoulders). They identify the proper distance to stand from "targets" (a slightly bent arm's length). They explain the importance of "kino escalation." (You must touch her. You must not be afraid to do this.) They are teaching the importance of subcommunication: what you convey about yourself before a single word has been spoken. They explain the importance of intonation. They explain what intonation is. "Your voice moves up and down in pitch to convey a variety of different emotions."

All of this is taught through a series of exercises. "This is going to feel completely artificial," says Jones on the first day of training. "But I need you to do the biggest shit-eating grin you've ever made in your life." Sarah is standing in the corner with her back to the students—three Indian guys, including one in a turban, three Chinese guys, and one Cambodian. The students have to cross the room, walking as an alpha male walks, and then place their hands on her shoulder—firmly but gently—and turn her around. Big smile. Bigger than you've ever smiled before. Raise your glass in a toast. Make eye contact and hold it. Speak loudly and clearly. Take up space without apology. This is what an alpha male does.

Before each student crosses the floor of that bare white cubicle in midtown, Tran asks him a question. "What is good in life?" Tran shouts.

The student then replies, in the loudest, most emphatic voice he can muster: "To crush my enemies, see them driven before me, and to hear the lamentation of their women—in my bed!"

For the intonation exercise, students repeat the phrase "I do what I want" with a variety of different moods.

"Say it like you're happy!" Jones shouts. ("I do what I want.") Say it like you're sad! ("I do what I want." The intonation utterly unchanged.) Like you're sad! ("I . . . do what I want.") Say it like you've just won $5 million! ("I do what I want.")

Raj, a twenty-six-year-old Indian virgin, can barely get his voice to alter during intonation exercise. But on Sunday night, on the last evening of the boot camp, I watch him cold-approach a set of women at the Hotel Gansevoort and engage them in conversation for a half-hour. He does not manage to "number close" or "kiss close." But he had done something that not very many people can do.

**OF THE DOZENS OF ASIAN-AMERICANS** I spoke with for this story, many were successful artists and scientists; or good-looking and socially integrated leaders; or tough, brassy, risk-taking, street-smart entrepreneurs. Of course, there are lots of such people around—do I even have to point that out? They are no more morally worthy than any other kind of Asian person. But they have figured out some useful things.

The lesson about the Bamboo Ceiling that James Hong learned from his interviewer at IBM stuck, and after working for a few years at Hewlett-Packard, he decided to strike off on his own. His first attempts at entrepreneurialism failed, but he finally struck pay dirt with a simple, not terribly refined idea that had a strong primal appeal: hotornot.com. Hong and his cofounder eventually sold the site for roughly $20 million.

Hong ran hotornot.com partly as a kind of incubator to seed in his employees the habits that had served him well. "We used to hire engineers from Berkeley—almost all Asian—who were on the cusp of being entrepreneurial but were instead headed toward jobs at big companies," he says. "We would train them in how to take risk, how to run things themselves. I remember encouraging one employee to read

*The Game*"—the infamous pickup-artist textbook—"because I figured growing the *cojones* to take risk was applicable to being an entrepreneur."

If the Bamboo Ceiling is ever going to break, it's probably going to have less to do with any form of behavior assimilation than with the emergence of risk-takers whose success obviates the need for Asians to meet someone else's behavioral standard. People like Steve Chen, who was one of the creators of YouTube, or Kai and Charles Huang, who created Guitar Hero. Or Tony Hsieh, the founder of Zappos.com, the online shoe retailer that he sold to Amazon for about a billion dollars in 2009. Hsieh is a short Asian man who speaks tersely and is devoid of obvious charisma. One cannot imagine him being promoted in an American corporation. And yet he has proved that an awkward Asian guy can be a formidable CEO and the unlikeliest of management gurus.

Hsieh didn't have to conform to Western standards of comportment because he adopted early on the Western value of risk-taking. Growing up, he would play recordings of himself in the morning practicing the violin, in lieu of actually practicing. He credits the experience he had running a pizza business at Harvard as more important than anything he learned in class. He had an instinctive sense of what the real world would require of him, and he knew that nothing his parents were teaching him would get him there.

You don't, by the way, have to be a Silicon Valley hotshot to break through the Bamboo Ceiling. You can also be a chef like Eddie Huang, whose little restaurant on the Lower East Side, BaoHaus, sells delicious pork buns. Huang grew up in Orlando with a hard-core Tiger Mom and a disciplinarian father. "As a kid, psychologically, my day was all about not getting my ass kicked," he says. He gravitated toward the black kids at school, who also knew something about corporal punishment. He was the smallest member of his football team, but his coach named him MVP in the seventh grade. "I was defensive tackle and right guard because I was just mean. I was nasty. I had this mentality where I was like, 'You're going to accept me or I'm going to fuck you up.'"

Huang had a rough twenties, bumping repeatedly against the Bamboo Ceiling. In college, editors at the *Orlando Sentinel* invited him to write about sports for the paper. But when he visited the offices, "the editor came in and goes, 'Oh, no.' And his exact words: 'You can't write with that face.'" Later, in film class at Columbia, he wrote a script about an Asian-American hot-dog vendor obsessed with his small penis. "The screenwriting teacher was like, 'I love this. You have a lot of Woody Allen in you. But do you think you could change it to Jewish characters?'" Still later, after graduating from Cardozo School of Law at Yeshiva University, he took a corporate job, where other associates would frequently say, "You have a lot of opinions for an Asian guy."

Finally, Huang decided to open a restaurant. Selling food was precisely the fate his parents wanted their son to avoid, and they didn't talk to him for months after he quit lawyering. But Huang understood instinctively that he couldn't make it work in the professional world his parents wanted him to join. "I've realized that food is one of the only places in America where we are the top dogs," he says. "Guys like David Chang or me—we can hang. There's a younger generation that grew up eating Chinese fast food. They respect our food. They may not respect anything else, but they respect our food."

Rather than strive to make himself acceptable to the world, Huang has chosen to buy his way back in, on his own terms. "What I've learned is that America is about money, and if you can make your culture commodifiable, then you're relevant," he says. "I don't believe anybody agrees with what I say or supports what I do because they truly want to love Asian people. They like my fucking pork buns, and I don't get it twisted."

**SOMETIME DURING THE HUNDREDS OF HOURS** Jefferson Mao spent among the mostly untouched English-language novels at the Flushing branch of the public library, he discovered literature's special power of transcendence, a freedom of imagination that can send you beyond the world's hierarchies. He had written to me seeking permission to swerve off the traditional ·path of professional striving—to devote himself to becoming an artist—but he was unsure of what risks he was willing to take. My answer was highly ambivalent. I recognized in him something of my own youthful ambition. And I knew where that had taken me.

Unlike Mao, I was not a poor, first-generation immigrant. I finished school alienated both from Asian culture (which, in my hometown, was barely visible) and the manners and mores of my white peers. But like Mao, I wanted to be an individual. I had refused both cultures as an act of self-assertion. An education spent dutifully acquiring credentials through relentless drilling seemed to me an obscenity. So did adopting the manipulative cheeriness that seemed to secure the popularity of white Americans.

Instead, I set about contriving to live beyond both poles. I wanted what James Baldwin sought as a writer—"a power which outlasts kingdoms." Anything short of that seemed a humiliating compromise. I would become an aristocrat of the spirit, who prides himself on his incompetence in the middling tasks that are the world's business. Who does not seek after material gain. Who is his own law.

This, of course, was madness. A child of Asian immigrants born into the suburbs of New Jersey and educated at Rutgers cannot be a law unto himself. The only way to approximate this is to refuse employment, because you will not be bossed around by people beneath you, and shave your expenses to the bone, because you cannot afford more, and move into a decaying Victorian mansion in Jersey City, so that your sense of eccentric distinction can be preserved in the midst of poverty, and cut yourself free of every form of bourgeois discipline, because these are precisely the habits that will keep you chained to the mediocre fate you consider worse than death.

Throughout my twenties, I proudly turned away from one institution of American life after another (for instance, a steady job), though they had already long since turned away from me. Academe seemed another kind of death—but then again, I had a transcript marred by as many F's as A's. I had come from a culture that was the middle path incarnate. And yet for some people, there can be no middle path, only transcendence or descent into the abyss.

I was descending into the abyss.

All this was well deserved. No one had any reason to think I was anything or anyone. And yet I felt entitled to demand this recognition. I knew this was wrong and impermissible; therefore I had to double down on it. The world brings low such people. It brought me low. I haven't had health insurance in ten years. I didn't earn more than $12,000 for eight consecutive years. I went three years in the prime of my adulthood without touching a woman. I did not produce a masterpiece.

I recall one of the strangest conversations I had in the city. A woman came up to me at a party and said she had been moved by a piece of writing I had published. She confessed that prior to reading it, she had never wanted to talk to me, and had always been sure, on the basis of what she could see from across the room, that I was nobody worth talking to, that I was in fact someone to avoid.

But she had been wrong about this, she told me: It was now plain to her that I was a person with great reserves of feeling and insight. She did not ask my forgiveness for this brutal misjudgment. Instead, what she wanted to know was— why had I kept that person she had glimpsed in my essay so well hidden? She confessed something of her own hidden sorrow: She had never been beautiful and had decided, early on, that it therefore fell to her to "love the world twice as hard." Why hadn't I done that?

Here was a drunk white lady speaking what so many others over the years must have been insufficiently drunk to tell me. It was the key to many things that had, and had not, happened. I understood this encounter better after learning about LEAP, and visiting Asian Playboy's boot camp. If you are a woman who isn't beautiful, it is a social reality that you will have to work twice as hard to hold anyone's attention. You can either linger on the unfairness of this or you can get with the program. If you are an Asian person who holds himself proudly aloof, nobody will respect that, or find it intriguing, or wonder if that challenging façade hides someone worth getting to know. They will simply write you off as someone not worth the trouble of talking to.

Having glimpsed just how unacceptable the world judges my demeanor, could I too strive to make up for my shortcomings? Practice a shit-eating grin until it becomes natural? Love the world twice as hard?

I see the appeal of getting with the program. But this is not my choice. Striving to meet others' expectations may be a necessary cost of assimilation, but I am not going to do it.

Often I think my defiance is just delusional, self-glorifying bullshit that artists have always told themselves to compensate for their poverty and powerlessness. But sometimes I think it's the only thing that has preserved me intact, and that what has been preserved is not just haughty caprice but in fact the meaning of my life. So this is what I told Mao: In lieu of loving the world twice as hard, I care, in the end, about expressing my obdurate singularity at any cost. I love this hard and unyielding part of myself more than any other reward the world has to offer a newly brightened and ingratiating demeanor, and I will bear any costs associated with it.

The first step toward self-reform is to admit your deficiencies. Though my early adulthood has been a protracted education in them, I do not admit mine. I'm fine. It's the rest of you who have a problem. Fuck all y'all.

Amy Chua returned to Yale from a long, exhausting book tour in which one television interviewer had led off by noting that Internet commenters were calling her a monster. By that point, she had become practiced at the special kind of self-presentation required of a person under public siege. "I do not think that Chinese parents are superior," she declared at the annual gathering of the Asian-American Students Alliance. "I think there are many ways to be a good parent."

Much of her talk to the students, and indeed much of the conversation surrounding the book, was focused on her own parenting decisions. But just as interesting is how her parents parented her. Chua was plainly the product of a brute-force Chinese education. *Battle Hymn of the Tiger Mother* includes many lessons she was taught by her parents—lessons any LEAP student would recognize. "Be modest, be humble, be simple," her mother told her. "Never complain or make excuses," her father instructed. "If something seems unfair at school, just prove yourself by working twice as hard and being twice as good."

In the book, Chua portrays her distaste for corporate law, which she practiced before going into academe. "My entire three years at the firm, I always felt like I was playacting, ridiculous in my suit," she writes. This malaise extended even earlier, to her time as a student. "I didn't care about the rights of criminals the way others did, and I froze whenever a professor called on me. I also wasn't naturally skeptical and questioning; I just wanted to write down everything the professor said and memorize it."

At the AASA gathering at Yale, Chua made the connection between her upbringing and her adult dissatisfaction. "My parents didn't sit around talking about politics and philosophy at the dinner table," she told the students. Even after she had escaped from corporate law and made it onto a law faculty, "I was kind of lost. I just didn't feel the passion." Eventually, she made a name for herself as the author of popular books about foreign policy and became an award-winning teacher. But it's plain that she was no better prepared for legal scholarship than she had been for corporate law. "It took me a long, long time," she said. "And I went through lots and lots of rejection." She recalled her extended search for an academic post, in which she was "just not able to do a good interview, just not able to present myself well."

In other words, *Battle Hymn* provides all the material needed to refute the very cultural polemic for which it was made to stand. Chua's Chinese education had gotten her through an elite schooling, but it left her unprepared for the real world. She does not hide any of this. She had set out, she explained, to write a memoir that was "defiantly self-incriminating"—and the result was a messy jumble of conflicting impulses, part provocation, part self-critique. Western readers rode roughshod over this paradox and made of Chua a kind of Asian minstrel figure. But more than anything else, *Battle Hymn* is a very American project—one no traditional Chinese person would think to undertake. "Even if you hate the book," Chua pointed out, "the one thing it is not is meek."

"The loudest duck gets shot" is a Chinese proverb. "The nail that sticks out gets hammered down" is a Japanese one. Its Western correlative: "The squeaky wheel gets the grease."

Chua had told her story and been hammered down. Yet here she was, fresh from her hammering, completely unbowed.

There is something salutary in that proud defiance. And though the debate she sparked about Asian-American life has been of questionable value, we will need more people with the same kind of defiance, willing to push themselves into the spotlight and to make some noise, to beat people up, to seduce women, to make mistakes, to become entrepreneurs, to stop doggedly pursuing official paper emblems attesting to their worthiness, to stop thinking those scraps of paper will secure anyone's happiness, and to dare to be interesting.

*New York Magazine, 2011*

# 3

## EDDIE HUANG AGAINST THE WORLD

**ON A COLD, DARK STREET IN TIJUANA, MEXICO,** I asked Eddie Huang a question that many people were sure to ask him in the months to come. "What did you expect?"

For the past week in December, Huang had been venting about his tortured ambivalence toward *Fresh Off the Boat*, the ABC sitcom based on the memoir he wrote about growing up as a child of Taiwanese immigrants in Orlando, Florida. He deployed his gift for pithy, wounding invective against the show's producers and writers — before professing gratitude and love for the same people he just vilified. He described what he took to be the show's falseness and insensitivity to nuance—before praising its first episode as the best sitcom pilot he had ever seen. He lamented the choice he had made to sell his life rights to a major network—before insisting that the premiere of *Fresh Off the Boat* on February 4 would be a milestone, not just in the history of television but in the history of the United States.

He had a point. *Fresh Off the Boat* would be the first network sitcom to star an Asian-American family in twenty years and only the third attempt by any major network in the history of the medium. Huang chose to sign with ABC in deference to the residual power of network television to alter mass perceptions about race, and he had hoped to portray the Asian-immigrant experience without equivocation or compromise.

"What did I expect?" Huang responded. "I expected I could change things." He told me that he thought his story was powerful enough for ABC to allow him to tell it his way. "I thought that people in network television had their own conscience about things."

Huang, thirty-two, was dressed in an acid-wash denim jacket and a black fur hat with its earflaps folded up, which lent his large, round baby face a not-at-all-coincidental resemblance to a certain East Asian dictator. (Huang likes to give himself nicknames—Kim Jong Trill, the Rotten Banana, the Human Panda, the Chinkstronaut—all of which, like the name of his show, repurpose and reclaim slurs and stereotypes.) He was sitting on the back fender of a Vice Media van, in which a five-man crew was preparing its equipment to shoot. We were waiting for two young female marijuana dealers whom Huang would be interviewing for "Huang's World," the gonzo food and travel show he hosts for Vice.

He had, he admitted, been extremely naïve about the realities of network television. By way of explanation, Huang reviewed for me the string of previous triumphs that induced him to overrate his ability to set his own terms in the world. "You have to remember how unlikely all of this was. With BaoHaus, for instance," he said, referring to the basement hole-in-the-wall Taiwanese sandwich shop that took Huang to the forefront of a new generation of hip young New York chefs, "I had never worked in a New York City restaurant. I came out of nowhere. And I did it!" After a brief dalliance with the Cooking Channel, Huang started the Vice show, which at the time was called *Fresh Off the Boat*. "When had there been a television host with an identity like mine— a hip-hop Asian kid? I was the first! And the show was a huge success!" In 2013, he published a memoir, the story that Huang had always wanted to tell, and it became a national bestseller. "And so I said, 'We can do this one more time!' But network television wasn't what I thought it was."

Huang feels that by adulterating the specificity of his childhood in the pursuit of universal appeal, the show was performing a kind of "reverse yellowface"—telling white American stories with Chinese faces. He doesn't want to purchase mainstream accessibility at the expense of the distinctiveness of his lived experiences, though he is aware of how acutely Asian-Americans hunger for any kind of cultural recognition. "Culturally, we are in an ice age," he said. "We don't even have fire. We don't even have the wheel. If this can be the first wheel, maybe others can make three more."

Then, he added, "we can get an axle and build a rice rocket."

**THE STORY HUANG TELLS** in his memoir is one of survival and struggle in a hostile environment—a prosperous neighborhood in Orlando. Though the picaresque book is written in Huang's jaunty mash-up of hip-hop lingo and conspicuously learned references to American history and literature, it is also an extraordinarily raw account of an abused and bullied child who grows to inflict violence on others. The racism Huang encounters in Florida is not underhanded, implicit, or subtle, as it often is for the many Asians from the professional classes living in and around the coastal cities where the American educated elite reside. It is open, overt, and violent.

"Up North and out West, you have a bit more focus on academics, and there are accelerated programs for high-achieving kids," said Emery Huang, reflecting on the tumultuous upbringing he shared with his brother. "Down South, you've got football and drinking, and that's it. If you weren't fighting, you were a nerd and a victim." In response to this bullying, the Huang brothers did not conform to the docile stereotypes of Asian-American youths, in large part because of the influence of their father, Louis. A hardened, street-smart man, Louis had been sent by his own father to the United States to get him away from the hoodlums he had been running with in Taipei. "We wouldn't get in trouble with our dad if we got into a fight," Emery said. "We would get in trouble if we didn't win."

Huang's memoir records an unusual life trajectory: from tormented outsider, to angry adolescent who would twice be arrested on assault charges, to marijuana dealer, to high-end street-wear designer (under the "Hoodman" label, which eventually led to a lawsuit from Bergdorf Goodman), to corporate lawyer, to successful restaurateur. The book fixates on themes of pain and punishment. As a teenager, Huang was commanded by his father to kneel and bow to police officers after he was caught stealing from neighbors. Later, he would find himself surrounded by cops with guns drawn after he drove his car into a crowd of frat guys who were menacing him and several friends (after one of his own broke a window at their house).

At times, Huang comes across in his memoir as a dutiful son who admires and reveres his parents and feels the enormous weight of obligation to them—"I wasn't mad at my dad," he writes after being forced to remain kneeling on his asphalt driveway for several hours, "I deserved it"—and at others as an enraged teenager, rebelling against constant assaults on his self-esteem to which he was subjected in the home—he recalls "constantly being told I was a *fan tong* (rice bucket), fat-ass or waste of space." He finds in hip-hop a language for his alienation, citing Tupac Shakur's "Me Against the World" as the cathartic soundtrack of his youth. ("Our parents, Confucius, the model-minority [expletive] and kung-fu-style discipline are what set us off," he wrote. "But Pac held us down.")

In Los Angeles later in December, while driving with Huang in his canary-yellow Porsche Boxster to his Malibu apartment, I asked him what his parents thought of his portrayal of the abuse they inflicted on him.

"My parents have never acknowledged that it was abuse—because in their culture and their country it wasn't," he said. Huang believes that the psychological and physical harm that was done to him was largely a matter of context. "I think the abuse had extra meaning that I gave to it, because I saw that it wasn't happening to other kids." For a time, every Friday afternoon, Huang said, social workers would take him out of class to inspect him for cuts and bruises. "And I knew that I was weird and different and was made to feel like I had done something wrong, like there was something wrong with us."

The book proposal for *Fresh Off the Boat* was sent to publishers not long after an excerpt from Amy Chua's memoir, *Battle Hymn of the Tiger Mother*, appeared in the *Wall Street Journal*. The commercial prospects of Huang's proposal were almost certainly enhanced by this coincidence: Chua's book indirectly addressed the chief preoccupation of the American upper middle class—getting their children into top-tier colleges—and therefore generated one of the infrequent moments in which Asian-Americans aroused the fascination of the wider American public. Chua made Asian-Americans matter just long enough for Huang's proposal to sell as a counternarrative to hers.

The *Journal* excerpt, titled "Why Chinese Mothers Are Superior," gave what Chua would later claim was a misleading impression of the overall arc of her book, which chronicled the crisis that ensued when her younger daughter revolted against "Chinese" parenting methods that might seem "unimaginable—even legally actionable" to Western parents. But the marketing campaign, of which the excerpt was a part, appealed to an underlying (and not entirely unjustified) concern among white American parents that they had grown too indulgent toward their children. Huang found the book repellent. "She Kumon-ized our existence," he told me, referring to the popular Japanese after-school learning program. "This is something that fifty- and sixty-year-old Asians are still dealing with."

When I spoke to Huang's parents, they didn't deny his claims, but they emphasized that there was a cultural and generational gap. They were young at the time, they said, and they had reverted to parenting practices they saw in Taiwan. "I wanted to make them tough," his father said, "and I think that I did." Emery, however, claims that his brother's harsh depiction of their childhood in the book seemed "sugarcoated."

Still, Huang is quick to say that he never thinks of his parents as bad people. "I do think about getting hit, though," he said. "And I definitely am the way I am because of it. I am quick to react. I am quick to protect myself. I am very comfortable with people yelling at me. And I am very comfortable telling people exactly what I think. I am very comfortable getting personal."

THIS MIXTURE OF LOVE AND LOATHING toward parents will be familiar to generations of immigrants of every color, but Asian-Americans feel this tension with an unusual acuteness, in part because Confucian tradition is so explicitly directed toward the breaking of individual autonomy in favor of the demands of the family. This tension is compounded by the fact that, as a result of the federal Immigration and Naturalization Act of 1965, which eased national-origin quotas, Asians began arriving in the United States in large numbers just as the cultural upheaval of the 1960s was drastically loosening American manners and mores. Today the means that many Asian-Americans apply to achieve academic success (a narrow emphasis on rote memorization and test preparation) could not be more out of step with the attitudes and practices of the socially liberal elite that Asians aspire to join. The ensuing cultural dissonance generates an awkward silence around the topic of Asian-Americans—Asian-Americans don't want to portray their parents as backward, and white liberals don't want to be seen as looking down on people of other races and cultures whose parenting practices seem primitive. Huang hates this silence.

It is no paradox that Huang's brazen attitude resembles nothing so much as that of his brash immigrant mother. As we arrived at his apartment in Malibu, Huang casually mentioned that his mother had on more than one occasion turned the wheel of her car sharply into oncoming traffic to terrorize her children into compliance. But Huang would later insist that he owes everything he has become to her. "Every morning, whether it was weekdays or weekends, she would get me up and start demanding: 'What are you going to do with yourself today? What is the plan? What is the itinerary?'" Huang credits this with instilling in him the drive that made him relentless in his pursuit of success.

In fact, his mother's haranguing inadvertently helped jump-start his writing career. In 2010, his attempt at a second restaurant, Xiao Ye, received a zero-star review in the *New York Times*. The restaurant's menu included facetiously racist items, including an "Everything but the Dog Meat Plate" and "Princeton Review Bean Paste Noodles." In the write-up, Sam Sifton lamented that "if Mr. Huang spent even a third of the time cooking that he does writing funny blog posts and wry Twitter updates, posting hip-hop videos and responding to Internet friends, rivals, critics and customers, Xiao Ye might be one of the more interesting restaurants to open in New York City in the last few months." Huang's blog went viral when he published an email his mother sent him after the review came out.

"Trust me, you much keep your bar license active just in case you need it," his mother wrote. "You do not even understand your own strength or the whole scope of this business, and you are not even willing to listen. YOU MUST GET BURNT BEFORE YOU WILL HEAR YOUR MOM. Please calm down, analyze yourself, and be honest. You have a lot of potential, but you must make good choice and stick to it with the best choice. With all the staff, and your korean friend, no one was able to point out or warn you the mistakes, or problems you have?????????????????????"

Huang closed the restaurant after repeat visits from the State Liquor Authority, which might have been peeved by his "Four Loko Thursday" deal, when the high-alcohol, caffeinated beverage was sold at a steep discount. (Huang had also floated the idea of an all-you-can-drink deal.) But Sifton grasped something important in his observation that the blog posts and Twitter updates mattered more to the chef than the food did. Huang's true ambitions always had more to do with writing than with feeding people. He told me he opened the restaurant "because no one wanted to listen to me."

Huang's cocky social-media personality kept getting him in trouble, but it only seemed to swell his fame. His inability to censor himself, combined with his talent for speaking frankly and intimately to a mass public, aligned him perfectly with the mood of social media. When the Cooking Channel signed Huang to host a show called *Cheap Bites*—the kind of opportunity that most dedicated chefs would hold on to for dear life — the deal fell apart after Huang lashed out at the network's biggest stars on Twitter. Huang has no regrets about the dust-up. ("The show looked like trash.") He was later named a TED fellow, a potential gateway into the world of highly compensated corporate speaking, but quickly got himself booted from the program when he skipped some of the events to appear on a podcast with the graffiti artist David Choe and the porn star Asa Akira. Choe declared it to be a meeting of the "worst Asians in the universe." Huang would later denounce TED as a "cult."

Huang's utter lack of instinct for self-preservation has had the curious effect of preserving himself against any harm. While the established institutions he railed against had myriad vested interests to balance and secrets to hide, Huang has always taken the inherently sympathetic role of the only honest man, refusing to compromise with arbitrary or corrupt authority. This has made Huang a particularly good fit with Vice Media, whose food channel, Munchies, seeks to appeal to young hipsters turned off by bourgeois "foodieism" but interested in educating their palates. Tricked out in big sunglasses, high-top sneakers, and flashy street wear, Huang's on-screen persona often resembles an Asian Ali G— easy to mock, were it not a deliberate self-caricature. Much of the pleasure of Huang's Vice show comes from watching him slyly emerge from his buffoonish character to make incisive comments revealing an agile, literary mind—and then lapse back into the role of the pot-addled numbskull.

I MET HUANG IN LOS ANGELES during a time of high tension surrounding his show, a few weeks after he exploded in a Twitter tirade, accusing the network of neutering his book, and a week before shooting would wrap. The executive producers were, at this point, careful to emphasize that the show was not a biography of Eddie Huang and his family. It was a loose adaptation "inspired" by, rather than "based" on, Huang's book. The series borrows the setting and the characters but applies them to a plot that was invented almost entirely by a professional writing staff, led by the showrunner Nahnatchka Khan. Though Huang lived the life depicted in the show, 20th Century Fox Television (which produces the show for ABC) retains creative control over it.

Melvin Mar, the producer at Fox who bought the rights to the book, told me that Huang's arrangement with the studio is atypical. Usually, a production company will pay an author for a book it options and neither seek nor offer further participation. But Huang insisted on being brought on as a producer as a condition of the sale. So, Mar told me, "we decided we would all do this together, like a family."

More than anything, the fraught dynamic that emerged between Mar and Huang resembles that of Huang's actual family. The ambivalence Huang feels toward his parents tends to manifest itself in all his dealings with authority, Mar most emphatically not excepted. Huang sometimes describes Mar as a mentor, someone who has taught him about when to pursue confrontation and when to acknowledge the necessity for accommodation. But these sincere expressions of respect often segue quickly to contempt for the compromises endemic to the entertainment industry. "It's a system that is kind of similar to the Asian upbringing," Huang told me. By giving up so much autonomy for his career's sake, Huang said, Mar "got a second set of parents in network television."

Mar and Khan met at a symposium for Asian-Americans interested in the popular arts, where they dealt with a familiar crowd of activists demanding to know why Hollywood seemed so uninterested in casting people who looked like themselves. (Mar's family is from China; Khan's is from Iran.) "You go to these conferences, and there's always people saying, 'You should do more for Asian people,'" Mar said. "And my response is, 'Yes, I agree with you.' But it's easier said than done. I have to bring actual projects that are viable and convince the executives that there's a real business case for making it."

The business case for making an Asian-American show is simple: Asian-Americans are the fastest-growing ethnic group in the country, they earn and spend more than the average American, and they are overrepresented in the advertiser-coveted eighteen-to-thirty-four-year-old demographic. But if the case were really so strong, surely two decades would not have passed without some network making a bid for this audience. Perhaps the reason is that the so-called Asian-American demographic (some 18 million viewers) is actually made up of many different nationalities with no common culture or language.

Moreover, comedies about nonwhite people generally must navigate a trap-laden path between offending the group represented and neutering the comedy to avoid doing so. And they suffer from having to be approved and produced by people who are overwhelmingly white, and thus unfamiliar with the nuances of the stories they are telling, and also intensely wary of giving offense — but all this does is increase the likelihood that these shows will be dull, though still capable of offending their audience. This is exactly what happened to *All-American Girl*, the sitcom starring the comedian Margaret Cho and the last significant attempt to make an Asian-American TV show. The series was disowned by the Korean-American community that it tried to portray and was eventually rejected by the wider audience for being unfunny. It was canceled after just one season, two decades ago.

*Fresh Off the Boat* was meant to be different. Not only is the production staff diverse, but the source material helps indemnify the show against criticism of many of its outlandish elements, which are rooted in Huang's actual life. For example, the ferociously uninhibited and heavily accented mother portrayed in the series might appear to be an offensive caricature if it were a generic "Tiger Mom" conjured out of thin air.

In fact, Constance Wu, the actress who plays Jessica Huang on the show, told me that she underplays her character in relation to the actual woman. "I don't actually think they would believe she was real," Wu said. "That's what reality television is for—to show you people who no one would actually believe were real." To preserve the appearance of reality, the show has had to depart from it—while also claiming that same reality as its license to go as far as it does in presenting a raw slice of immigrant life.

**WHEN MAR ASKED KHAN** to sketch out her vision for the show, she described what would become the opening scene of the series: a tight focus on someone in hip-hop garb that pulls out to reveal . . . a short, chubby Asian boy. The apparent incongruity (more apparent than real) is at once a joke for the prime-time network audience and a wedge that protects the series from recapitulating "model minority" representations of Asian-Americans. It is also the sore point that offends Huang more than any other aspect of the show.

Hip-hop had been the emblem of Huang's alienation from his own household and the violence he encountered at school. It provided a language through which to reject the role of the eager assimilator that his own culture seemed to urge onto him. It was, as Huang described it in his book, a means of survival—not some glib, touristic fascination, or even a way of being cool. Huang identified with the black kids at school because they, too, were enduring beatings in their households in a way that white kids weren't. "It's a funny position being an Asian in America," Huang wrote. "You're the dude who can cross the union line. Your community actually wants you to sell the [expletive] out and work in law, accounting or banking. But I realized then that I wasn't going to cross the picket line." (Though he was briefly a corporate lawyer.) "I was down with the rotten bananas who want nothing to do with that."

Huang's appropriation of the language of racialized resistance might seem intrinsically noncredible to many white, black, and even Asian interlocutors, who—implicitly or explicitly— regard Asian-Americans as the minority group that gets ahead by working hard and eschewing the politics of racial grievance. Not Huang, who likes to analogize his relationship with Mar to that of the "field Chinaman" to the "house Chinaman." (Mar called this comparison "height-

EDDIE HUANG AGAINST THE WORLD ◇ 75

ened," which was his diplomatic way of saying "fantastically overwrought." If there is a class distinction between the two men, it's this: Mar's family worked in the bean-sprout business in Los Angeles's Chinatown, while Huang's father become a millionaire many times over in Orlando.)

Huang especially took issue with the second episode in the series, in which a youthful Eddie develops a protosexual fascination with a blond, large-breasted trophy wife who has just moved into the neighborhood. It includes a scene in which Eddie fantasizes himself into a rap video. He "makes it rain" and squirts Capri Sun onto models. Though test audiences found the scene to be innocuously funny, Huang considered the thrust of the episode outright offensive. In his estimation, it denigrates hip-hop culture by portraying it as a vector for adopting sexist attitudes—a perversion of what, for him, had been a vital emotional outlet. His analysis is credible but, as the writers and producers told him, *way* too abstruse for anyone in the audience to think about.

"It's so interesting, what he's going through," Khan told me. "Most people never get the opportunity to experience what he's experiencing. So now he's rebelling and manifesting the angst, and that's what makes him him, and that's why he wrote the memoir in the first place. Part of me just wants to say, 'Sit back and enjoy this.'"

When I told Huang that Khan wanted him to sit back and enjoy the ride, he had an immediate response: "That's what pedophiles tell children."

Even if Huang's attraction to black culture is played for cheap laughs, to him it is an essential element of his person. It provides the missing half of the fully human entity that the Asian-American who consents to the model-minority myth has to relinquish. A model minority is a tractable, one-dimensional simulacrum of a person, stripped of complexity, nuance, danger, and sexuality—a person devoid of dramatic interest. Huang is something else: a person at war with all the constraints that would fetter him to anything less than an identity capacious enough to contain all his contradictions and ambivalence.

AT THE HOTEL ON OUR LAST DAY IN TIJUANA, Huang spent the morning managing his Manhattan restaurant, Baohaus, by Skype. Besides traveling twenty-four weeks of the year for Vice, writing a second memoir, and working on the ABC series, Huang continues to manage his restaurant. He often finds himself in fights with one cook in particular, an older Cantonese-speaking veteran of Chinatown restaurants. Huang is as exacting as a boss as he is insubordinate as an employee, but he is often forced to suffer the rebelliousness of his staff. He and the cook argued about how to properly cut chicken. The cook wanted to slice the chicken, which he believed white people prefer. Huang wanted it done the proper way, diced. "He never really accepts what I tell him," he said. "And as soon as I turn my back, he starts doing it his own way."

"I've wanted to fire him so many times," he said. "The problem is, you can't teach American kids the speed this guy has or his ability to problem-solve on the fly."

As he thought about it, Huang hit on a comparison between Hollywood executives and the typical Chinatown restaurant. Both, he said, think they know what people want and strive to give them exactly that. But it never occurs to either of them to sell people the authentic thing itself— Chinese food the way Chinese people make it for themselves or, in the case of Hollywood, stories that don't rely on formulaic contrivance to be funny.

"I really feel that people don't always know what's good for them," he said. "When you have a strong conviction, you have a duty not to tell people what they want. At least represent yourself and say: 'Yo, this is what I'm into, and this is what I'm seeing in the world. Let me take your hand and guide you through it, so you can see through my eyes.'"

*New York Times Magazine, 2015*

# PART II

## 4

# THE LIFE AND AFTERLIFE OF AARON SWARTZ

**YEARS BEFORE HE HANGED HIMSELF** in his Crown Heights apartment, the hacker, writer, and activist Aaron Swartz used to debate with his then-girlfriend Quinn Norton whether the Internet would mourn him if he died. It was Swartz's stubborn belief that no one would notice or care if he died young, as he often thought he was fated to do. Like many young men of great promise and fluctuating moods, Swartz was an unstable compound of self-effacement and self-regard—among the most empowered, well-connected young people in America, yet convinced that his very existence was a burden to others, even those who loved him. Back when Aaron was twenty and the journalist Norton was thirty-three, before they had crossed over into a complicated romantic affair, Norton brought Swartz with her to a tech event in Berlin, where he and her ex-husband, the tech writer Danny O'Brien, played a game in which they tried to "kill" themselves on Wikipedia, seeing how long they could remain dead before some volunteer editor restored them to life. Neither could remain dead for more than ten minutes.

There is a category of young person able to do things like contribute to the building of the Internet in their teens, or sell their tech start-ups for millions of dollars when they are nineteen, or rally a million opponents to a major piece of legislation when they are in their twenties. Usually such people are not the same young people who write on their blogs that they are too frightened to ask for a glass of water on a plane, or that "even among my closest friends, I still feel like something of an imposition, and the slightest shock, the slightest hint that I'm correct, sends me scurrying back into my hole." Swartz was preternaturally adult when he was still a child and still a precocious child after he had grown to adulthood—"so vulnerable and fragile," his friend Ben Wikler said. "He put up shields in all the wrong places." He had done more in twenty-six years than most of us will do in a lifetime, but often avowed to others, and most of all himself, that he had done nothing of any worth at all.

By the time he was seventeen, Swartz had already secured a permanent legacy written in code. When he was thirteen, he was coauthoring a version of RSS, a system that allows streaming of news from across the Internet onto a single reader; in his later teens he helped to build and sell Reddit, a news message board that has grown into one of the world's most heavily trafficked sites, and created the coding backbone of the Creative Commons licenses that allow artists and writers to claim or waive certain rights to control their works or share them online—the coin of the realm for a growing community of progressive activists known as the copyleft movement, devoted to building an economy of culture based on sharing.

But he was also an ailing person in great physical and

emotional pain—a sufferer from ulcerative colitis and suicidal depression, which he described so vividly on his blog (once with enough specificity that a Reddit colleague had the police break down Swartz's door). Norton spent much of 2010 keeping Swartz away from suicide, telling him, she told me, "This, the way this feels, this is gonna calm down. Like when you get a little bit older, this is gonna be OK. It's not ever gonna go away completely, but it's gonna be something you can manage." As he confessed on his blog in late 2007, he was not merely ailing, he was also ashamed to bear the stigma of his illnesses, and the shame made it difficult to treat both of his conditions. "To some degree I was kind of like, 'Stop making me deal with this,'" Norton told me. "'Stop making me the only one who knows.'"

The progressive activist Taren Stinebrickner-Kauffman, who began dating Swartz in the summer of 2011, after he and Norton had broken up and just before the federal indictment for hacking MIT's JSTOR academic-article database that would define the last year of his life, knew a more securely grounded boyfriend than Norton had—one who was beginning to learn that "direct confrontation was often not the best way," that participating in electoral politics might be more effective than in-the-shadows hacktivism, and who was doing the dishes for the first time in his life. He had assured her that the depressive episodes described in his blog were a thing of the past, and she says that nothing in his conduct gave her cause to doubt it. The first time she ever worried about his depression, she told me, was on the morning of January 11—the day she would discover him hanging from his belt in the apartment they shared.

The sanctification of Aaron Swartz began immediately—first online, then off. He had become a millionaire from the sale of Reddit to Condé Nast, but then turned his back on Silicon Valley for good to become an intellectual adventurer, teaching himself economics, sociology, history, and psychology by dropping into the lives of experts, as he well understood that any minimally informed admirer can do. He still worked on projects to organize and make available information online, but was increasingly intent on finding the secret to mobilizing masses to political action. Swartz was one of the early catalysts for the campaign that stopped the Internet regulation known as the Stop Online Piracy Act (and its corollary, the PROTECT IP Act), which its opponents believe would have effectively allowed private companies to censor the Internet. During this campaign, which was waged while Swartz was still facing indictment, he emerged as a leader who occupied a position of unusual credibility and authority. And it was this transition, from a builder of platforms for machines that do precisely what you tell them to do to freelance scholar-activist poised to intervene in the messier realm of democratic politics on behalf of Internet culture, that made so many think of him, even at twenty-six, as the kind of person who, as the writer and activist Cory Doctorow wrote when he died, "could have revolutionized American (and worldwide) politics."

At his funeral in the Chicago suburb of Highland Park, where he was born and raised, the hundreds of mourners were a mix of members of family and Aaron's far-flung networks, including some towering figures who had known Aaron since he was a chubby kid. There was Tim Berners-Lee, who invented the World Wide Web, and the Harvard professor Lawrence Lessig, eminence among Internet legal theorists, each channeling the cosmic sorrow and worldly rage already circulating online before a packed crowd of mourners clad in black, the men wearing kippahs.

First, there was remembrance of the person Swartz had been, full of adoration and tenderness and a kind of exasperated love for how preternaturally wise he could be and how mundanely stupid. Then there was remembrance of the circumstances under which he died—as an accused felon prosecuted by the U.S. Attorney of Massachusetts for the crime of downloading too many (4.8 million) academic articles from an online archive hosted by MIT, an extravagant gesture motivated by the cause of using technology to liberate culture from corporate ownership. After two years of exhausting negotiations, which had taken him no closer to an acceptable plea bargain, Swartz was three months from the start of his trial when he preempted it, and his legal plight loomed large in the way all of those around him understood his death. "Aaron did not commit suicide," said Robert Swartz, Aaron's father, "but was killed by the government."

In rhetorical salvos like these, at the funeral in Highland Park and at the vigils held in Cambridge and New York and San Francisco and Washington, D.C., Swartz emerged as a human repository of the Internet's virtues and its unrealized fantasy of social transformation. Again and again, his friends made the point that Swartz's open-access activism was merely the prologue to his truly immodest ambition to "hack the whole world," and to realize his dream of "a world without any injustice or suffering of any kind." His closest friends and family were keen to reject any effort to "pathologize" Swartz's condition, though he had himself described it as sickness. "Aaron was depressed because God is depressed," said Lessig at his funeral. "Look at this world and what we have done—who wouldn't be depressed?"

"I'VE HEARD A LOT OF PEOPLE TALK ABOUT Aaron's impossibly high standards and youthful enthusiasm and naïve brilliance," said his friend and executor, Alec Resnick. "I can't help but think that the whole point of people like Aaron is to show us how low and base and hidebound our expectations are."

Those expectations were largely formed by his early life as a young prodigy raised among idealists. One day, when he was three years old, as Robert Swartz recounted to the funeral audience, Aaron asked his mother: "What was this 'Free Family Entertainment in Downtown Highland Park'?" "She asked him, What was he talking about?" A volley of laughter issued from the audience. "He said, 'Mom, it says here on the refrigerator.' He had taught himself to read."

He built a working ATM in the third grade—it distributed coupons and tracked student accounts. He created a Wikipedia-like site at thirteen, leading to introductions to Berners-Lee and others who shared the view on Internet advertising he shared then with the *Chicago Tribune*: "That's not what the Internet was made for," he said. "It was based on open standards and freedom, not ads." He dropped out of high school after the ninth grade and spent his days in conversation with grown-up technologists, missing out on the numbing busywork and status anxiety that fills the days of American high-school students—depicted so memorably in the Highland Park films of John Hughes. "High school had been the most unpleasant experience of my life," said his father, who was supportive of Aaron's decision. "If things come easily to you, and you understand things quickly, you spend a lot of time in school bored out of your mind."

Robert Swartz is a compact, robust man with a ruddy face; he was a longtime owner of a small tech company and is now an intellectual-property consultant to, among other places, the MIT Media Lab. The company—which produced a Unix-like operating system—was named after his father, an entrepreneur and a nuclear-disarmament and peace activist who founded the Albert Einstein Peace Prize Foundation.

In interviews, Aaron Swartz described his childhood as lonely and his suburb as a place without a center. In one of his early blog posts, Swartz had described Highland Park, not uncharitably, as one of the places where the parents were educated and well-meaning, and had looked upon the struggles for justice of the sixties with sympathy, though they did not themselves participate. It was a perfect place from which to escape into cyberspace; at a vigil at Cooper Union, Norton recounted a memory of Swartz singing Pete Seeger's "Little Boxes" to her daughter.

After emailing Lawrence Lessig a suggestion on how to design certain Creative Commons licenses in 2002, Swartz went to work with him on it, beginning one of the many long and complicated mentor relationships that seemed to fill Aaron's life. He enrolled briefly at Stanford University, incubator of tech entrepreneurs, despite never having finished high school (he was rejected by Berkeley), but left after a year for Paul Graham's unstructured tech think tank Y Combinator, having found Stanford intellectually unchallenging. By day four, Swartz had already concluded that Stanford was a kind of "libertarian nightmare world."

In the winter of 2007, after spending time with Norton in Berlin, Swartz's colitis flared up. He holed up in Boston for a week, AWOL from Reddit, which he had already stopped treating like a serious commitment—he was fired when he eventually did show up at the offices in San Francisco. That week in Boston, he posted a fictional account of a suicide, which described among other things his hatred for his chubby boy's body.

In 2009, Swartz took a monthlong vacation from the Internet—one of the first he had ever experienced. He wrote about it on his blog, which, when it wasn't summarizing a social-scientific controversy, or criticizing the work or motivations of previous collaborators, was exploring the conflicted inner life he was so good at keeping from others.

"I am not happy," he wrote. "I used to think of myself as just an unhappy person: a misanthrope, prone to mood swings and eating binges, who spends his days moping around the house in his pajamas, too shy and sad to step outside. But that's not how I was offline. I loved people—everyone from the counter clerk to the old friends I bumped into on the street."

Toward the end of the post, Swartz reflected on the extraordinary life he has lived, one made possible by the Internet, and his willingness to seize its possibilities.

"I realize it must seem like the greatest arrogance to think one could escape life's mundane concerns, like asking to live on a cloud, floating above the mere mortals," he wrote. "But it was that arrogance that made me think I could contribute to adult mailing lists when I was still in elementary school, that arrogance that made me think someone might want to read my website when I was still just a teen, that arrogance that had me start a company as a college freshman. That sort of arrogance—not bragging, but simply inwardly thinking I could do more than was expected of me—is the only thing that's gotten me anywhere in life."

"One of the things that makes him the Internet's boy is he was already living in the future that I hope we get to," said Norton. "Where everybody has the permission to act and be important and where hierarchies don't prevent people from doing things or believing in themselves and just having a fucking life. We get a huge number of messages that we are not allowed in the world. We occupy social laws of living, and we are not allowed to leave them. And all we ever have to do is walk out. And I think one of the most extraordinary, moving parts of Aaron's life, his story, is that he just didn't accept the limits that we put on ourselves."

In a blog post a few months later, Swartz engages in a brief philosophical inquiry into how a person can live a moral life. "The conclusion is inescapable: we must live our lives to promote the most overall good. And that would seem to mean helping those most in want—the world's poorest people." He would go on to specify which moral actors he found the most admirable. "Our rule demands one do everything they can to help the poorest—not just spending one's wealth and selling one's possessions, but breaking the law if that will help," he wrote. "It seems like these criminals, not the average work-aday law-abiding citizen, should be our moral exemplars."


SWARTZ WAS A FELLOW at the Lessig-headed Edmond J. Safra Center for Ethics at Harvard in September 2010 when he allegedly began the batch download that would lead to his arrest and indictment. Over the course of several weeks, the indictment claimed, Swartz engaged in a game of digital cat and mouse as first JSTOR, then MIT, sought to block his access to its network, causing JSTOR on two separate occasions to block all access to MIT computers for several days. Starting in November of that year, Swartz bypassed the wireless registration and plugged directly into the network from a closet on campus, hiding the laptop under a box and running a script to discover and download articles continuously.

The indictment alleged that Swartz was attempting to download the archive for the intention of sharing it online—perhaps carrying forward the agenda of the Open Access movement, which protested the locking away behind a paywall of academic articles. (He had taken a strong position on this issue with the online publication of the Guerilla Open Access Manifesto, a polemic written by Swartz and a small group of collaborators.) It charged him with wire fraud, computer fraud, unlawfully obtaining information from a protected computer, and recklessly damaging a protected computer. He faced up to $1 million in fines and up to thirty-five years in prison. The indictment was later amended to thirteen felony counts and as much as fifty years in prison. But those numbers are entirely notional; the plea-bargain phase settled on a reported offer of six to eight months if Swartz would plead guilty to thirteen felony counts. If he rejected the deal, as he did, the government would recommend a sentence as long as seven years if he was convicted.

Whether any of this constituted a crime that ought to have been one of society's priorities to punish depends on one's perspective. No harm had come of it besides a few days of hassle for the MIT IT staff, and, as is always true of digital reproduction, taking copies of JSTOR's archive left JSTOR with perfect copies of its own. JSTOR eventually made peace with Swartz when he returned the data, and the organization publicly announced it had no further wish to see him prosecuted. Though there were many efforts by the Swartzes to extract a similar statement from MIT, none came.

The analogy his supporters used to describe the crime was "checking out too many books from the library." The U.S. Attorney for Massachusetts put it differently: Swartz was a thief. It was the latest skirmish in a battle over which analogies would control the digital world—the resort to analogies being a sign both of how rudimentary the legal concepts that govern the Internet are and how slow a consensus is to form about a new medium.

This was a battle fought along many fronts; in legal journals and academic symposia, where a cadre of activists who nurtured Swartz in their midst tried to build a new consensus about who should and should not control the circulation of ideas; in the everyday practices of a hundred million Internet users, who had grown inured to sharing music and videos online; in the offices and laboratories of software and media companies, where the latest copy-protection schemes are devised in an ever-escalating arms race with those intent on undoing them; in the corridors of Congress, where lobbyists from the various media, old and new, seek advantage for their industries by shaping laws that reflect their economic interests; and in courtrooms, where those unlucky enough to be caught flouting the laws face prosecution for doing what the rest of us habitually do on the Internet—copy for free. Though its opponents had a stronger hold on the levers of power, the copyleft believed it possessed an unbeatable trump card: the future, in the form of everyone's children, who had grown up without any encumbrances on "content."

Swartz was one of those children, and his interventions began at the margins where the public right to information was unambiguous. In 2008, Swartz exploited a limited opening in the pacer court-document archive to download and release millions of records. The FBI investigated him but ultimately declined to prosecute.

At a memorial, Swartz's friend Carl Malamud confessed that he wondered if his own hot criticisms of JSTOR—he had tweeted that charging $20 for a six-page article was "morally offensive"—had incited Aaron to take undue risks in hacking it. When I spoke to him a week later, Malamud still hadn't answered the question for himself. I asked why he had said that he sometimes feels guilty.

"Because the boy got in trouble and he killed himself," he said. "Did I encourage him to do JSTOR? There were quite a few of us banging the table about this. Did we incite him to do this, and could we have done more once he was arrested? I don't know. I ask the questions, and I can't answer them. I can't look in somebody else's head and figure out what he was thinking. I could second-guess myself and ask what I did wrong, and I hope folks at JSTOR and MIT are doing the same. This was a tragedy."

Malamud described Swartz as having been "terrified" by the FBI investigation into the pacer download. Resnick recalls him worrying that the FBI was going to break down his door at any moment. And yet it didn't seem to deter him—he continued to plot and carry out hacktivist assaults on databases designed to withhold information behind a fairly steep paywall. As the law professor Orin Kerr pointed out to me on the phone, here was the truly puzzling juncture in the data-liberation career of Aaron Swartz. "Many people would take being investigated by the Feds and let off without charges as an occasion to become more cautious and not to see it as a green light to do even more," he said. "I would have told him not to do it, or else to do it if he wished, but to be aware that if he got caught, he was going to be prosecuted and he was going to face jail time."

Swartz, connected to the leading legal lights of the Internet, almost certainly knew that already. Even more perplexing was that, by all accounts of those who knew his thinking best, Swartz had been drawing back from hacker activism even before the JSTOR incident. He had shifted his focus to economic inequality and health care.

"This was emphatically *not* what he was spending his time thinking about," his friend Resnick said of the JSTOR hack. "At best it was a weekend project, which unfortunately went very wrong."

I asked Malamud how terrified Swartz could have been if the pacer episode didn't stop him from even a casual hacking of JSTOR. "I think he was still terrified, but he was also brave. He saw this as something that was right to do, and so he did it."

**THE MORALISTIC LANGUAGE** spoken by the Open Access movement—with its invocations of Gandhi, Martin Luther King Jr., and Rosa Parks—may seem slightly perplexing to those of us raised with the commonsense view that works of science, art, and culture circulate in our society through institutions that fund them by charging fees to the public to access them. But the partisans of the open Internet were informed by a different experience and set of ideals than the rest of us, those of a techno-utopia that really existed and has been continuously under siege ever since John Perry Barlow, the former Grateful Dead lyricist turned Internet visionary, cofounded the Electronic Frontier Foundation and declared the independence of cyberspace as a self-regulating realm of perfect freedom beyond the reach of any territorial government's laws.

That Swartz was a self-described hacker mattered greatly to his legal fate—through constant repetition in the media, many have come to associate the term with criminality, the breaching of restrictions on access, the stealing of secrets, even acts of espionage and cyberwarfare. But in the term's original incarnation at MIT, the hacker was a kind of monastic devotee of the computer who practiced a new kind of ethics calibrated to explore the new world it was creating.

Steven Levy, in his seminal book *Hackers,* neatly evoked the working principles that governed the hacker ethic:

"Hackers believe that essential lessons can be learned about the systems—about the world—from taking things apart, seeing how they work, and using this knowledge to create new and even more interesting things," he wrote. "They resent any person, physical barrier, or law that tries to keep them from doing this. . . . Imperfect systems infuriate hackers, whose primal instinct is to debug them. . . . In a perfect hacker world, anyone pissed off enough to open up a control box near a traffic light and take it apart to make it work better should be perfectly welcome to make the attempt. Rules that prevent you from taking matters like that into your own hands are too ridiculous to even consider abiding by."

The book describes all the hacker rule-breaking that unfolded in the MIT artificial-intelligence labs, with hackers crawling through the vents, stealing and making unauthorized copies of keys, to get access to the tools they needed for their explorations. Administrators at MIT have been dealing with, and indulging, such spirited rule-breaking for decades. MIT hacks usually involve some inventive mischief in the physical world, such as affixing parlor furniture to the underside of a campus archway, or stealing the Caltech cannon and transporting it across the country. No one is arrested or imprisoned for what everyone understands is an exercise of the high spirits of brilliant young men who earn their indulgence by being members of a technological elite at an elite institution. MIT hackers breach security to test their powers, to repay the insult of keeping them out, and never for base personal gain, never in order to steal credit-card numbers like some computer-enabled foreign thug. And yet the laws that keep out the Russian mob invariably end up prohibiting much of what the hackers do. And therein lies the tension: between the rules that can and should govern elite cadres of monastic devotees of knowledge in itself and the rules that can be applied to society at large. The sharing ethos confined to the MIT artificial-intelligence lab was a great boost to technological progress; but released into the world, it has produced waves of innovation and disruption about which it takes a nearly religious faith to trust that they will all result in outcomes that will be better for everyone.

WHEN I MET Taren Stinebrickner-Kauffman in Brooklyn, she broke down only once during an hour-long conversation, when we came to the subject of what happened to Swartz's case on the day he died. Just that afternoon, his attorney, Elliot Peters, was making a consequential discovery. There had been a puzzling thirty-four-day delay between the arrest and the request for a warrant to search Swartz's laptop— longer than the prosecution is allowed. And information that Peters recently received from the U.S. Attorney's Office was strengthening his bid to suppress the searches from that laptop in court. "We were all excited about this," said Peters, "and I was already thinking of how I was going to cross-examine them, when I got this email from Bob Swartz saying Aaron had committed suicide."

"If only Aaron had waited another week or so," Stinebrickner-Kauffman said, her face crumpling into tears. The family and their intimate supporters were gearing up for a public fight. The tagline would have been "Save Aaron," the slogan accompanying it "Nerd does not equal criminal."

But Stinebrickner-Kauffman had already begun to sense the "aversion and cringing" that overtook Swartz when he had to start asking people for money. His fear of being a burden on others, his horror of being made the center of attention, were interfering with his preparation for his own defense.

In order to defend himself, he would have had to confess to everyone that he had made a boneheaded miscalculation that had made him into the imposition on everyone's time and money that he always feared that he was. He would have to admit that the ailing, depressed, imperfect shadow side of him was just as real as the brilliant, precocious, successful, morally exemplary side that everyone was celebrating.

"I remember talking to him about this; I told him that for someone with such clear vision about so much, one blind spot he had was how much he mattered," said Wikler. "Aaron took his life in another small room with bare white walls. He couldn't hear our voices at that moment."

"He had this thing about not being able to bring yourself to do things you don't want to do," Stinebrickner-Kauffman said. "Everybody has to do things that they don't want to do. And we all know that it's really annoying and maybe even painful. But those kind of things were even harder for him than for most people." Swartz had said that he would rather spend the rest of his life without a fixed residence, sleeping on other people's couches, than work at an office job that he did not want to take. "He occupied a higher plane where everything was thinking and writing and doing and meeting with people who were really interesting and smart. And he filled as much of his life as possible with that, far more than anybody else I know. But when it came to having to do something that he didn't want to do, he couldn't do it."

In the end, he didn't want to be the martyr he has become. The suicide that eventually thrust him into that role was also an attempt to evade it, by evading trial. A weekend side project on an issue he didn't even care that much about anymore was keeping him firmly ensnared in the past, and might even blot out the new life he was entering.

"I used to tell him the most important thing was never to get caught," said Norton. "I know these people and I know what they are capable of." Toward the end of their relationship, Swartz and Norton began to part company on their view of the American political system, which Norton saw as irredeemably fallen and which Swartz had come to believe was preferable to others, in part because it allowed technocratic elites like himself to play an outsize role. "I swear to God that boy just wanted to live inside an episode of *The West Wing*," she said. "He wanted to find the halls of power and do his earnest best to make everything a little bit better. And I just believed that was a dead end. And I felt like one of the tragedies of this whole story is that he proved me right." Among the reasons Swartz turned down the plea bargains, Wikler told me, was that a felony would constrain him from having the kind of life he now wanted: "You can't be secretary of commerce," he said, with a felony conviction. Early on, after his arrest but before his indictment, Swartz was offered an unusual deal—one count of violating the Computer Fraud and Abuse Act and three months in jail. He turned even that down.

François de La Rochefoucauld once observed that it's not enough to have great virtues; one must use them with economy. As I listened to the tributes to Aaron Swartz in Highland Park and New York and online, this aphorism came to mind. Swartz had skipped out on the lessons taught by the American high school—the lessons in cynical acquiescence, conformity, and obedience to the powers that be. He was right to think these lessons injure people's innate sense of curiosity and morality and inure them to mediocrity. He was right to credit his "arrogance" for the excellence of the life he lived. But if nothing else, these lessons prepare people for a world that can often be met in no other way; a world whose irrational power must sometimes simply be endured. This was a lesson that he contrived never to learn, which was part of what made him so extraordinary. It was Swartz's misfortune, and ours, that he learned it too late, from too unyielding a teacher. It cannot serve society's purpose to make a felon and an inmate out of so gifted and well-meaning a person as Aaron Swartz, and thus he was a victim of a grave injustice. But it bears remembering that the greater injustice was done to Aaron Swartz by the man who killed him.

*New York Magazine, 2013*

# 5

# THE LIVELIEST MIND IN NEW YORK

**"IT'S A BIT OF A STRUGGLE** to get comfortable right now," says Tony Judt, who is seated in a book-lined office in an apartment above Washington Square. He says this in a matter-of-fact way. He has been resting a little, as he does for short spells throughout the day. The room is very warm and quiet, save for the whirring of the air pump that keeps his diaphragm functioning and his labored intake through the bipap valve embedded in each of his nostrils. Three large computer monitors stand adjacent to one another on a long desk. They run a looped slideshow—snapshots of Judt walking with his wife, clowning around with his children, wearing various styles of glasses (square and clunky giving way to round and sleek), sitting in a chair with an arm draped casually across its back.

Now Judt excuses himself and very patiently gives instructions on how to make sitting upright, for a time, bearable. *Just a little bit forward with the legs, please. All right. Now—up—and back.* His nurse, a sturdy man with a black ponytail, wrestles with the electronic knobs that control the many moving parts of his wheelchair. *No—up, as far as it can go. Far as it can go. That's right. Just a little bit down. And now back. That's right.* Judt requires the assistance of a microphone to be easily heard, and the speaker crackles with the sound of his sighs.

The disease that has paralyzed most of Judt's body— amyotrophic lateral sclerosis, or Lou Gehrig's disease—has reduced his voice to a hoarse whisper, though it still retains the distinctive rhythms and intonations that made it, until recently, a commanding instrument. Judt is, by common assent, one of the most eloquent and erudite public intellectuals working today—"one of the great political writers of the age," in the judgment of the political philosopher John Gray. He presides over the Remarque Institute at New York University, where he supports research, schedules lectures, and shapes the direction of European historical studies. He has written eight books on the history of politics and ideas in Europe, and is a famously tough-minded and combative writer of essays, reviews, and op-ed pieces. All in all, he is one of the most admired and denounced thinkers living in New York City.

ALS is incurable, fatal, and little understood. It leaves its victims mentally intact. It does not obliterate sensation, and it does not inflict any pain. As Judt puts it, "You're free to sit there quite calmly contemplating your own steady decline." Recently, he dictated for a short essay offering his readers a glimpse into his bedroom at night. "There I lie," he wrote, "trussed, myopic, and motionless like a modern-day mummy, alone in my corporeal prison, accompanied for the rest of the night only by my thoughts."

He went on to invite his readers to imagine deleting their ability to move their arms and legs from various daily settings—to scratch their hand, or shift position at night— and consider the effect this would have on their morale. Morning, he wrote, brings "an occasion to communicate with the outside world and express in words, often angry words, the bottled-up irritations and frustrations of physical inanition." By the time he refers to his "cockroachlike existence" of "humiliating helplessness," his simple thought experiments have posed a paradox: How can a man enduring the unbelievable torment described within the essay have retained the clarity and poise to have written it?

The essay was unlike anything he had written before: an intimate view of the author's private anguish. "I can't remember another piece of memoiristic writing that created such waves of interest in our little pond," says the writer and Columbia professor Todd Gitlin. It was not, however, the whole of his written output. After spending a few months absorbing the shock of his diagnosis eighteen months ago, Judt has become enormously prolific: dictating essays and opinion pieces, delivering a public lecture to a packed auditorium, and assembling material for three books, one of which—a rallying cry on behalf of a renewed social democracy—will be published next week. Consigned to a broken body but perfectly sound in mind, he has acquired something of a second presence beyond that of a historian and public intellectual—a figure whose pathos haunts the thoughts of others. "There are many days now where I find myself thinking about Tony Judt," says Gitlin, "and I hardly even know him."

"I use words to make sense of my life," explains Judt.

"Words can make the illness a subject I can master, and not one that one simply emotes over." Longtime admirers believe Judt's writing is stronger than it has ever been. "He has been able to do some of his best work," says Robert Silvers, the editor of the *New York Review of Books*, who has assigned Judt more than sixty pieces over the years. "The pure intensity of effort and courage needed to arrive at the ability to do it is something difficult to imagine. It's a great victory for him."

Judt politely declines to entertain any suggestion that there is something heroic in what he has accomplished. "It's not heroic. Heroism consists of doing things you don't have to do and that cause you tremendous cost that you're willing to accept in order to do the thing you feel you have to do. It doesn't cost me anything to write. Where I do think I deserve merit points is for sheer strength of will. The natural thing to do is to say 'fuck it'—to lie down with a whiskey and watch old movies. It takes willpower to say, 'I'll be happier if I do this than if I just lie there, bored.' "

Judt's academic reputation rests on the 2005 publication of *Postwar: A History of Europe Since 1945*. It was an enormous success: The Yale historian Timothy Snyder, who is collaborating with Judt on a follow-up book, calls *Postwar* "the best book on its subject that will ever be written by anyone"; Louis Menand, reviewing the book in *The New Yorker*, wrote that Judt's scope was "virtually superhuman." *Postwar* recounts two related stories: how Western Europe banished political extremism by building a robust welfare state, and how Eastern Europe first succumbed to and later released itself from communist rule. The book hinges on a series of painful ironies, each of which Judt pins down with precision.

He both exposes the self-serving myth of European resistance to the Nazis during the war and acknowledges that it was precisely on the basis of such myths that a ruined Europe was able to restore itself. He also observes that because war, genocide, and ethnic cleansing had separated the fractious, ethnically diverse regions of Eastern Europe into tidy, homogeneous nation-states, "the stability of postwar Europe rested upon the accomplishments of Josef Stalin and Adolf Hitler."

Judt regards himself as a teller of hard, impolite truths. "I've always been willing to say exactly what I think," he declares. To wit: His own NYU history department used to be mostly "dull and p.c."; most other historians are unable to write "to save their lives"; and public intellectuals who aren't an expert in something are "blah-blah generalists—and then you're David Brooks. And you're garbage."

In his writing, Judt has a way of electrifying the atmosphere around intellectual debates, flinging shards of rhetoric sharp enough to shatter myths. Among his targets over the years: communism, the postmodern academy, French intellectuals, fellow liberals, fellow Jews. In 2006, he published an article in the *London Review of Books* accusing the American liberal intellectual class—singling out by name David Remnick, Peter Beinart, Leon Wieseltier, Michael Ignatieff, and Paul Berman—of a collective abdication of their critical responsibilities, calling them "useful idiots" of the Bush administration. In response, dozens of liberals who had opposed the war signed a manifesto denouncing the piece as "nonsense on stilts."

To some extent, Judt's Iraq essay could be read as payback for the sharp exchanges that had occurred three years earlier in response to another bombshell he had thrown. In an infamous article in titled "Israel: The Alternative," Judt declared, "The depressing truth is that Israel today is bad for the Jews." For Israel to remain a Jewish state, he wrote, it would be all but impossible to remain a democracy: The demographics of "Greater Israel" (which includes an overwhelmingly Arab population in the occupied territories) will soon make this logically impossible. Yes, Israel could dismantle its settlements, but this appeared to Judt a fantasy: "Many of those settlers will die—and kill—rather than move." Or Israel could forcibly expel its Arab population, "but at the cost of becoming the first modern democracy to conduct full-scale ethnic cleansing as a state project." The alternative Judt floated was to establish Israel as a binational state—in effect, to give up on the Zionist project entirely.

Upon its publication, Judt was branded, as he puts it, as "a crazed, left-wing, anti-Zionist and self-hating Jew," stripped of his contributing editorship at the *New Republic* and labeled by Leon Wieseltier, his close friend and the editor there, as someone who had called for "the abolition of the Jewish nation-state."

This is not a particularly helpful sobriquet for a Jew living in Manhattan, and Judt disputes the characterization of his essay (he was describing an emerging reality, he says, not advocating a solution). But to "think the unthinkable," as he urged his readers to do about Israel's future—and to say it aloud—has been Judt's self-assigned mission. "I think intellectuals have a primary duty to dissent not from the conventional wisdom of the age (though that too) but, and above all, from the consensus of their own community," he says.

"So liberals should look especially hard at the uninterrogated assumptions of liberalism. Otherwise we are just hacks for a party line. If I have an Archimedean ethical standpoint, it really just consists of telling the truth as I see it even if I don't much care for the implications, or if it offends my friends and my political allies."

Judt is a man of many commitments and loyalties, none of them unconditional, and all of them subservient to the preservation of intellectual independence. "I grew up among Marxist autodidacts, but was never a root-and-branch Marxist for that very reason," Judt explains. "It's like chicken pox: If you're inoculated early enough, you don't get it completely." In the sixties, he spent his summers working on a kibbutz, but he now says he was "never entirely, wholeheartedly 'part of the project.'" This sense of dislocation followed him to Cambridge, where he studied and taught for twelve years yet never quite belonged. "At a certain point," he says, "to remain slightly tangential to wherever I was became a way of 'being Tony': by not being anything that everyone else was."

In the spring of 2008, the neuromuscular disease that was already stirring in Judt began sending out its first faint warning signals. While typing, he would slip and hit the wrong key, "as if your fingers wouldn't quite do what you had told them to do." Judt had undergone treatment for sarcoma in his left arm only six years earlier, and the prospect of another devastating illness was not on his mind. "Next thing you know," he says, "you're throwing a baseball and it doesn't go quite as far as you expected, and you're still thinking, 'Oh, shit, I'm getting old.' And then you go for a walk and your breathing is a bit tight, and you think, 'I need to work out more.' And it's only when the doctor puts all these things together do you realize, 'Wait a minute, what's happening here is more serious.' "

ALS causes the neurons that connect the brain to the spinal cord and the spinal cord to the muscles to degenerate. The brain loses the ability to control movement. The muscles atrophy and die. Judt was diagnosed in September 2008, and the rapid deterioration of the large muscles in the lower part of his body set in soon afterward.

"He always wanted to continue doing things until it was no longer possible," says Casey Selwyn, a recent NYU graduate who worked as Judt's assistant. "Things like turning pages, or typing, or using a mouse." She watched as, one by one, these faculties faltered. "Until it was absolutely physically no longer possible," she says, "he would keep doing it."

Before his diagnosis, Judt had just begun imagining his next magnum opus, a follow-up to *Postwar* that would trace the history of twentieth-century social and political thought. These plans fell by the wayside—"Reality is a powerful solvent," he says—and in November 2008, the Yale historian Timothy Snyder proposed, in its place, that they collaborate on a series of interviews ranging across the breadth of Judt's career.

The disappointment was painful—Judt had never worked with a collaborator before—but he was impressed with Snyder's intellect, and the partnership has been successful. "So long as your collaborator is very talented," Judt allows, "it's great fun."

Their discussions took place against the backdrop of Judt's rapid decline. By January 2009, he had lost the use of his arms. By March, his legs began to fail. He was on a respirator by May. "Without actually saying 'You'll be dead next month,'" Judt remembers, "the doctors said, 'This is very fast. It's unusual.'" Every week for five months, Snyder interviewed Judt for hours on end. "We wanted to get enough material for Tim to finish up on his own in case I was not able to do it with him," Judt says.

Soon after they finished their project, in May, a remarkable thing happened: Judt's health stabilized. The large muscles in most of his body were long gone, but the small muscles that control eating, speaking, and swallowing remained unaffected. They could go at any time and take him with them, or they could last a long time—months, even years. No one knows why his body stopped degenerating, or what happens next.

The interview sessions with Snyder awakened in Judt the urge to start writing again, and to make some noise. In June, he returned to print for the first time since his diagnosis with an op-ed in the *Times* warning that if Obama failed to follow through on his call for a settlement freeze in the occupied territories, "the United States would be humiliated in the eyes of its friends, not to speak of its foes." In July, he wrote a eulogy for the left-wing Israeli journalist and historian Amos Elon in the *New York Review of Books* contending that Zionism has, "for a growing number of Israelis, been corrupted into an uncompromising ethno-religious real estate pact with a partisan God." Here was the old Tony Judt, renewing the old polemics. He was not backing down an inch.

"I would say that I have become more radical as I have gotten older," he says. "I started out very radical when I was young, like most people, but I became less actively politically engaged in the middle of my life. And now I detect—and I don't just think it's because I have ALS—an urgency about the need to be angrier about what needs doing, what needs saving, and what needs changing."

In a sense, it is Judt's continued engagement with the world that has kept him sane. In order to pass the time at night, he has trained himself to enter into prolonged reveries: He organizes various memories into "a Swiss chalet," placing certain thoughts in certain cupboards, and different examples in different shelves. The mnemonic device has worked well enough that he can wake in the morning and dictate the first draft of brief autobiographical essays, which he would send as emails to friends. They are now published as a series in the *New York Review of Books* and will eventually be collected into a short book.

Some of the essays are charming reminiscences on light subjects such as his mother's dismal British cooking. Recently, they have begun to dip, as if by the gravitational pull of Judt's temperament, into ever more polemical forays. One recent essay on the dangers of identity politics assailed "para-academic programs" like gender studies and Asian-Pacific-American studies that "encourage members of that minority to study *themselves*—thereby simultaneously negating the goals of a liberal education and reinforcing the sectarian and ghetto mentalities they purport to undermine."

In "Kibbutz," Judt wrote about his youthful infatuation with Israel and his eventual disillusionment following the Six-Day War, when he learned, to his chagrin, that "most Israelis were not transplanted latter-day agrarian socialists but young, prejudiced urban Jews who differed from their

European or American counterparts chiefly in their macho, swaggering self-confidence, and access to armed weapons."

Ever since his friend Edward Said died in 2003, Judt has been assigned, not without his own participation, the mantle of the most visible intellectual dissident from the American consensus on the Israeli-Palestinian conflict. The subject of Israel's fate upsets him greatly. "It's true I feel something between a kind of sorrow and anger that that country is going in that direction," he says. "I feel I want to stamp hard on the toes of my fellow Jews and ask them: Have you any idea what kind of a place this is that you blindly defend?" He holds in greatest disdain those American Jews who have come down hard on his stance on Israel while declining to live there themselves. "The people whose necks hurt when I write about the Middle East tend to live in Brooklyn or Boca Raton: the kind of Zionist who pays another man to live in Israel for him. I have nothing but contempt for such people."

In August of last year, Judt found himself planning out the agenda for the Remarque Institute. He told the dean of NYU that he intended to give a seminar about social democracy— its problems and its prospects today. In response, the dean suggested he consider making it a public lecture.

Samuel Johnson famously likened women preachers to dogs walking on their hind legs: "It is not done well; but you are surprised to find it done at all." As the audience gathered at the Skirball Center at NYU one night last October—nearly 1,000 people, including much of New York's intellectual community—there was considerable unease in the air. It was Judt's first major public-speaking engagement since his diagnosis. Would this famously articulate speaker, rumored to be afflicted by a dreadful sickness, even meet the John-sonian standard?

"We did not know what to expect," says the Columbia University historian Istvan Deak, who had collaborated with Judt in the past. "We were worried about whether he would be able to speak at all, and how painful it would be to see this terribly ill man." Judt himself knew that his mental capacity was undiminished. Still, he would be unable to take a drink or be adjusted if his body grew uncomfortable, and the logistics of having someone join him onstage to turn the pages of his notes were tricky enough that he decided to memorize the entire lecture. "It would have to be a pure adrenaline-driven performance," he remembers.

After a fulsome introduction by the dean, Judt was wheeled onto the stage, accompanied by his breathing apparatus and swaddled in a black blanket. He looked ancient and regal and slightly unearthly; his head was clean-shaven, his nostrils distended by the bi-pap valves. Alone onstage, Judt had only two resources to draw on: his words and his will. But they were sufficient to keep the crowd enthralled.

Judt delivered a masterful performance, speaking for an hour and a half without interruption or hesitation. He began by referring to himself as "a quadriplegic wearing facial Tupperware," and, after running through a concise history of his illness, declared, to an enormous upsurge of laughter and applause, "What you see before you is an original talking head." As he turned to the substance of his speech, Judt's voice grew stronger, spontaneously generating the same seamless structure of well-ordered thought that he had habitually produced before his illness. "Why is it," he asked the audience, "that here in the United States we have such difficulty even imagining a different sort of society from the one whose dysfunctions and inequalities trouble us so?"

Judt left the auditorium satisfied: He had delivered as vigorous a cry for the importance of old-fashioned left-wing ideas as had been heard in New York in some time. ("It was a good lecture by any standard," he says, "not just the standard of quadriplegics with bi-paps.") Afterward, in his apartment, Judt elaborated on the themes of his speech. "There is much more to be done," he said, "in defense of what we used to think of as classical philosophical abstractions—justice, fairness, equality—in countries like the United States which have become increasingly unjust, unfair, unequal, and which are, by their nature, intuitively unworkable over the long run. If we say it's not fair that Goldman Sachs can rip off the taxpayer, we are told that that is a silly way to talk and that it has nothing to do with fairness. Well, it has everything to do with fairness. You can't run a society that is profoundly unfair for a long time without people becoming profoundly distrustful, and without social trust, there can be no common consent and no common goods, and no shared purposes. We need to find a way to once again talk about these things, in ways that used to be commonplace, but now have become radical propositions."

The speech has had a prolonged afterlife. It was published in the *New York Review of Books* last December, and Judt worked quickly to expand it into a longer essay, which then aroused the interest of the Penguin Press, who encouraged Judt to expand it further. Judt calls the resulting book, *Ill*

*Fares the Land,* "an essay on the possibility of living differently." It was rushed to press, and will be released next week.

It has been a long time since such a political pamphlet has found an American audience. "Who knows if I can get a readership for a book like that," he says. "But if I don't try, I have no right to complain that no one is reading or writing such things." Judt acknowledges the degree to which his illness has added to the curiosity surrounding his work. "I am a little caught between satisfaction at my newly increased reach and mild irritation at the reason for it," he says. "I understand the sense in which it seems as though I am in a hurry. But as you'll see when you read the book, I am quite convinced that the urgency lies in the external world and all I am doing is drawing attention to it."

"You're going to find this weird," Judt says, "but the thing I do best is teach." He considers his role as teacher to be more important than his work as a historian or public intellectual, and he has received hundreds of letters from former students over the years expressing their gratitude. Last spring, Judt taught an undergraduate class in his living room, and since then he has continued to teach a graduate seminar and the occasional individual student.

One Wednesday last month, as a blizzard blankets Washington Square, Judt is helping a second-year graduate student, whom we will call Gabrielle, construct a dissertation reading list on Jewish history.

Gabrielle is a fresh-faced woman in her twenties who speaks with a French accent. They settle into an easy rapport, readily interrupting each other and finishing each other's sentences.

"So, how many books . . ." asks Gabrielle.

"Should we do in toto? Look, if the choices are between twenty, fifty, a hundred, and five hundred . . ." Judt begins.

"We go for five hundred?"

"We go for one hundred, dear," Judt replies. "There won't be more than a hundred books worth reading."

Their talk ranges across the whole of European Jewish history—Eastern, Central, and Western Europe, the Sephardim, the "port Jews" living in places like Salonika and Alexandria. They arrange to meet weekly to plow through the reading.

"I have a request," Gabrielle mentions. "I said yes to a seder in California. I'll be away for just four days, but I feel guilty."

"Guilty toward the work or guilty toward me? That's why God created holidays. So people like you can go to California."

After a while, they turn to more personal subjects. "I cannot resist Cambridge people," Gabrielle confesses.

"That's a bad basis on which to select anything—husbands, boyfriends, whatever," says Judt with an amused nod of the head.

"I know!" Gabrielle says ruefully, shrugging.

"I had the same problem once, with midwestern Puritans, with similar consequences."

They laugh. "All right, then, kiddo. You have your marching orders."

After Gabrielle leaves, and in the remaining interval before his massage therapist arrives, Judt talks about focusing his unsentimental mind on the subject of his own illness. He gives the impression that rationality is sufficient to master any situation. When a reporter for the *Guardian* asked him recently if he would ever consider euthanasia, he answered without hesitation. "It's perfectly reasonable that there will come a point where the balance of judgment of life over death swings the other way."

It is the fate of every strong, indomitable personality to confront his or her own decline, and no one, it seems, has done so with harder lucidity than Judt. "Nothing prepares you to die," he says. "I imagine it helps if you are profoundly religious, if you absolutely, unequivocally believe that there is a purpose to all this, and that you are going to go somewhere nice. I don't believe either of those things.

"I thought of this as a stroke of catastrophic bad luck," Judt explains. "Neither unjust, because after all, there is no justice in luck; nor unfair—'Why me and not you?'—which would be a ridiculous way to think of it; nor implausible, because it's so implausible that plausibility is off the scale. Nor does it have meaning: One thing I always felt very strongly empathetic about in my reading of [the Italian chemist and Holocaust diarist] Primo Levi was his absolutely clearheaded sense that none of what had happened to him in the camps had any meaning. You might draw lessons from it in terms of experience, you certainly might draw political lessons. But at the existential level of one man's life, it had no meaning. *This has no meaning.* What I do with it is up to me.

"History can show you that it was one pile of bad stuff after another. It can also show you that there's been tremendous progress in knowledge, behavior, laws, civilization. It cannot show you that there was a meaning behind it. And if you can't find a meaning behind history, what would be the meaning of any single life? I was born accidentally. I lived accidentally in London. We nearly migrated to New Zealand. So much of my life has been a product of chance, I can't see a meaning in it at all. I can just see the good stuff that happened and the bad stuff.

"The meaning of our life," Judt continues, "is only incorporated in the way other people feel about us. Once I die, my life will acquire meaning in the way they see whatever it is I did, for them, for the world, the people I've known. I have no control of that. All I can do is do the best, now."

*New York Magazine, 2010*

# 6

# THE TERRORIST SEARCH ENGINE

EVAN FRANÇOIS KOHLMANN acquired his unloved nickname in 2002, when an FBI agent who was consulting with him on a case dubbed him "the Doogie Howser of Terrorism." The many detractors he has amassed over the years have never let go of that memorable handle. "Look," Kohlmann says one afternoon earlier this year, sitting in the two-bedroom apartment where he spends his days and nights analyzing jihadist video, communiqués, and chatter on the Internet. "Someone gave me that nickname when I was twenty-three years old. I'm not twenty-three anymore. How old do I have to be before they stop it?"

The nickname is one of the reasons observers are inclined to underrate Kohlmann, who is thirty-one. The outlandish but true story he tells—of Islamist revolutionaries spreading out from Afghanistan to wage holy war around the globe—is one you would expect to hear from a toffee-colored man with an Oxbridge accent, or a ruddy man with a buzz cut and no neck. You would not expect to hear it from Kohlmann, who is wearing, when I meet him, a close-fitting spandex biking shirt, black jeans, and Tevas. "It also doesn't help that I look about ten years old," he observes.

But jihad is a subject that has fascinated Kohlmann since he was eighteen. He has served as the government's expert witness in seventeen terrorism cases in the United States and nine abroad, making him the most prolific such expert in the country. He is hired to educate juries on the history and structure of Al-Qaeda and on the methods it uses to finance itself and recruit new members. He is very effective on the stand. "Evan has succeeded because he is the best in that particular business," says Thomas Hegghammer, a respected jihad historian at the Norwegian Defence Research Establishment. Kohlmann's testimony has helped to convict twenty defendants in U.S. federal courts and in the military commissions in Guantánamo Bay.

Kohlmann's indispensable font of evidence is the web. Since soon after 9/11, he has been arguing that the Internet is not only helping terrorists organize but is also serving as a recruitment tool to turn jihad sympathizers who have no connection to Al-Qaeda into terrorists themselves. This notion once seemed eccentric, but over the past year "homegrown terrorists," radicalized on the Internet, have appeared with regularity on the front page of the world's newspapers. The U.S. government has targeted for assassination Anwar al-Awlaki, an American-born Yemeni cleric whose exhortations to holy war, delivered in perfect English, are widely traded online. Al-Awlaki was directly in contact with Major Nidal Malik Hasan, a military psychologist who went on a killing spree at Fort Hood, and Umar Farouk Abdulmutallab, who attempted to detonate explosives in his underwear in a flight over Detroit last Christmas. Roshonara Choudhry, a twenty-one-year-old British woman, stabbed a British M.P. after downloading and listening to more than a hundred hours of Al-Awlaki's sermons. Mohamed Osman Mohamud, the nineteen-year-old who was arrested last month for allegedly attempting to detonate a bomb at a Portland, Oregon, tree-lighting ceremony, submitted articles to the online jihadist magazine *Inspire*. And then there was the strange case of Jihad Jamie and Jihad Jane—two white American women who traveled to Europe last year in an alleged plot to murder an artist who had offended Muslims.

Over the summer, it was reported that both the CIA and Google had invested in a company that trawls the jihadi Internet for "open source intelligence." This was a tacit acknowledgment of the value of what Kohlmann and a small group of like-minded private-sector analysts have been doing for more than a decade. "Evan's usually one of the first on the scene when something is breaking," says Jarret Brachman, the former research director of the Combating Terrorism Center, based at West Point. "You can't deny a record of analytic success. I really thought he was ahead of the curve on the emergence of Al-Qaeda in the Arabian Peninsula, for instance." Kohlmann watched online as AQAP, as terrorism researchers call it, transformed from a regional concern to an organization with international ambitions. (AQAP is likely responsible for the explosives packed into printer cartridges that grounded cargo flights in October.)

And yet Kohlmann's analytic successes have continued to be shadowed by controversy—and for reasons more significant than his youthful appearance. Kohlmann has, for the past seven years, made his living as an expert witness for hire during an episode of American history that posterity may record as not among its proudest. Our criminal-justice system, chastened by its failure to take the 9/11 hijackers seriously before they struck, has greatly expanded the share of prospective terrorist threats that it treats as real. While this aggressive posture may well have contributed to the absence of any major attack since 9/11, it has also produced a raft of cases that tend to look more frightening at the initial press conference than they do once evidence is admitted at trial, and situations in which the only terrorist plots the defendants have participated in are those invented by the government.

To his admirers, Kohlmann is just the kind of indefatigable obsessive we need to track down the fanatics who confront us. But by agreeing to testify in the trials of nearly every defendant placed before him, Kohlmann has earned a reputation among many scholars as a "hand for hire," as London School of Economics professor Fawaz Gerges puts it, working in the "guilty-verdict industry." Another leading terrorism scholar calls him a "whore of the court," making basic analytical errors on the stand and engaging in a charade of expertise. It is the opinion of George Washington University constitutional-law professor Jonathan Turley that Kohlmann was "grown hydroponically in the basement of the Bush Justice Department." Kohlmann says he simply testifies to what he sees on the web—and what he sees frightens him very much.

OVER THE PAST DECADE, Kohlmann has patiently assembled one of the world's largest collections of jihadi material—

terabytes' worth of sermons, *fatwas,* newsletters, message-board discussions, and video. Especially video: hundreds of hours of terrorist-training camps, martyrdom wills, live footage from the battlefields of Iraq and Afghanistan, beheadings, explosions, and burned bodies. He has catalogued this material for easy retrieval by law-enforcement agencies hoping to match a name to a face or producers looking to illustrate a television-news report. The videos have names like *Russian Hell in the Year 2000, Parts I and II, Martyrs of Bosnia,* and *The Destruction of the USS* Cole. They are sophisticated media productions at the outer limit of human extremity, and they are Kohlmann's daily bread.

"I oftentimes get to know the people that I'm studying . . . better than I know members of my own family," Kohlmann once testified. The demands of his work and the odd hours he spends on the Internet have eliminated his social life. "I never go out," he tells me from his home office in the meat-packing district. Once, when he brought a woman home, she was startled to find herself surrounded by dozens of pictures of bearded jihadists. She pointed at the image of Abu Hamza al-Masri, the disfigured London-based radical cleric who has hooks for hands, and told him, "You've got to take that guy off your wall."

Kohlmann loads a video for me of a man building a bomb and narrates it in the high-octane vernacular he uses to good effect in court and on TV. The video, he explains, was released last fall, not long after the arrest of Najibullah Zazi, who planned to set off a bomb in Manhattan. "Najibullah Zazi was trying to pull off some kind of bomb plot involving nail-polish remover. So the other day, somebody goes on the forum and posts this homemade video which shows you how to produce the explosive that Zazi was trying to produce, except using all homemade ingredients. This here shows you how to produce a very powerful explosive using things you can buy at Duane Reade.

"Now, let's say instead of building a bomb, you want to build a rocket. Like, for instance, there were guys down in South Carolina who were captured by the police with materials in their trunk that looked like they wanted to build a Qassam-style rocket. Well, it turns out that this guy has already very helpfully produced a video on how to produce rocket propellant. Again, it was posted on this forum saying, 'Guys, you should do this. We can all do this. Look—I've done it.'" Kohlmann clicks on another file, pulling up another image of the same person in a different setting. "There. Look—it's the same guy, once again, now producing rocket propellant. There's the rocket right there!"

These videos are discussed in online jihadist magazines like *Inspire* and *Jihad Recollections* and distributed on sites like that of Muntada al-Ansar—where Al-Qaeda in Iraq released images of IED attacks on American soldiers—and Ansar Al-Mujahideen, the English-language message board where the Pakistani Taliban meet and greet their American fan base. Kohlmann discerns a strange intimacy emerging among the forum members, whether they're in Afghanistan or the American suburbs. They reinforce one another in their beliefs and emphasize the importance of taking action. "Certain people start saying, 'Well, if you support this so much, isn't it your duty to join this?'" Though the members have never met in person, they develop ties with their message-board brothers possibly stronger than any they have with the people in their real lives. "And that's when we start seeing people posting messages saying, 'Look, guys, I love you, you're wonderful, but I can't sit here anymore. I've got to go out into the real world; I've got to go where death and destruction truly are.'"

In February, Kohlmann delivered a speech at the Center on Law and Security at New York University in which he portrayed a handful of recent terrorist scares as vindication. "I've had a lot of conversations over the last few years about recruitment shifting from the mosque and community center to the Internet, and a lot of people told me I was crazy or had an insular view on this," he told the audience. Kohlmann then went on to relate the story of a suicide bombing that occurred at Camp Chapman near Khost, Afghanistan, in December, in which Humam al-Balawi, a thirty-two-year-old Jordanian doctor, entered a CIA base, presumably as an informant. Instead, he blew himself up, along with seven CIA agents. "The disturbing part about this doctor is that we knew about Humam al-Balawi. Not in December or November. We'd known about him for years. He was famous," said Kohlmann. "He was famous on the Internet.

"Abu Dujana al-Khorasani, as he was known on the Internet forums, posted messages saying, 'I'm going to Afghanistan. I'm going to fight there. I'm going to kill Americans.' He said in an online Taliban magazine, 'No matter how much they pay me, what they do to me, what threats they make, I'll never give up this struggle. I'll continue in this until I reach my mission.' At that very moment, the CIA believed that he had been recruited as an informant. He was saying this in public, openly."

In his apartment, Kohlmann relates the excitement that the revelation of Al-Balawi's identity touched off. When the Pakistani Taliban identified the bomber by his online nom de guerre, he was astonished. "I nearly . . . my mouth hung open. I said, 'I know who this guy is!' At first I said to myself, 'It can't possibly be the same guy from the forum, can it? It can't possibly be that guy.' And sure enough, the forum participants were the first people who picked up on it, and said, 'Oh my God, that's our friend.' "

**KOHLMANN OWES HIS TERRORISM EDUCATION** to a think tank called the Investigative Project on Terrorism (IPT), where he began work as an intern in 1998, during his freshman year at Georgetown. IPT was founded by Steve Emerson, a former journalist who spent the nineties warning of the Islamic-militancy threat and assailing a Middle Eastern–studies establishment inclined to mince words over whether Islamic militancy deserved the label "terrorism" at all. He was a polarizing figure, regarded as an Islamophobe alarmist by many—he famously described the 1995 Oklahoma City bombings by Timothy McVeigh as exhibiting a "Middle Eastern trait"—but credited for paying attention to the threat of Islamic terrorism when others were inclined to downplay it. Prior to 9/11, he had the ear of top White House counterterrorism official Richard Clarke, who has written that Emerson would provide him information on jihad that he could not get out of his own intelligence agencies.

Emerson, together with a handful of other polemicists such as Daniel Pipes and Martin Kramer, built a network of think tanks devoted to disseminating a hawkish view of the Middle East conflict they found missing from within the academy. The mutual distrust that arose between these two groups has created a curious gap in our knowledge of Islamic militancy in America. "Broadly speaking, among the people who have the knowledge of language, culture, and history, there is little interest in studying security issues because it's seen as politically compromising and tied to a pro-Israeli or pro-government agenda," explains Hegghammer, one of Kohlmann's few defenders in academe. Hegghammer notes that a decade after 9/11, not a single professor at an Ivy League university specializes in jihadism. "And conversely, the people who do study security issues tend not to have the languages and culture. And so the people that wind up doing it tend to be fringe figures."

September 11, 2001, was Kohlmann's first day of law school at the University of Pennsylvania. When he heard the news, he got up to leave, telling the student sitting next to him, "This was an attack by Osama bin Laden, and I have to go do something about it." Kohlmann remained affiliated with IPT through 2003, eventually assuming the title of senior terrorism researcher. Around that time, government prosecutors began to look for help in explaining global jihad to juries. Middle Eastern studies professors tended to be reluctant to testify, but the researchers affiliated with the Emerson wing of counterterrorist studies were already gathering open-source information that corroborated the government's views of the threat. This is how a twenty-five-year-old law student turned out to be among the best-qualified people prosecutors could find who was willing to take the work.

Part of what arouses the ire of Kohlmann's critics is that his years with Emerson are his only formal credential. Kohlmann does not speak Arabic; has never been to Iraq or Afghanistan; does not hold a postgraduate degree in any related field; has no experience in military, law-enforcement, or intelligence work; and continues to submit—seven years into his career as a court-appointed expert on Al-Qaeda—his undergraduate thesis on Arab mujahideen in Afghanistan as evidence of his expertise. And yet judges continue to certify him, in large part in deference to previous judges and because of the weight that prosecutors place on his testimony.

"If they had other options, don't you think they would take them?" he asks me. "The only reason I get these jobs is the fact that I do them properly." Kohlmann can make up to $125,000 a year as an expert witness, and even more as a government consultant. These are not his only sources of income, but they are easily the largest.

THE CASE OF MOHAMED OSMAN MOHAMUD, the alleged would-be Oregon bomber, is similar to many in which Kohlmann testifies. The FBI affidavit paints a picture of Mohamud as a genuine threat—and perhaps the evidence presented in court will bear this out. But as the government emphasized in its public announcement of the charges, Mohamud never posed an actual danger to anyone other than himself.

Many post-9/11 terrorism prosecutions rely on a series of statutes prohibiting any "material support" offered to terrorism, a broadly sweeping term with vaguely defined limits. Under traditional conspiracy prosecutions, the government has to show that a defendant knowingly participated in planning to commit a crime. Under the material-support statutes, which were strengthened by the 2001 Patriot Act, the government has to show only that a defendant knowingly gave support to an individual or foreign group that has been designated as a terrorist entity, regardless of whether there was any intent to aid a terrorist act. "The statutes are like a utility infielder for prosecutors," says Stephen Vladeck, a law professor at American University's Washington College of Law. It lowers the bar for what the government has to prove, and it is invoked whenever the conduct charged is not clearly criminal under other statutes.

The material-support statutes help the government solve a thorny constitutional problem: How do you use the courts, which are designed to punish prior conduct, to preempt terrorist acts before they happen? One recurring solution has been to launch terrorism prosecutions in which no criminal plans are even alleged—because the plot is fictitious and created by the government. In these sting operations, the government uses paid informants or undercover agents to tempt defendants into convoluted schemes to either commit terrorist acts or provide material support to terrorist organizations. The informants befriend their targets and encourage their grievances. They enable them with financial and logistical help. In many cases, they secure only ambiguous assent.

Mohamud's terrorist plot was initiated by FBI agents who had worked on the sting operation for six months. Last week, Attorney General Eric Holder told reporters he is "confident that there is no entrapment here." Mohamud volunteered to informants that he had submitted articles to *Inspire* and *Jihad*

*Recollections,* and his statements leave no doubt that he was a believer in holy war against American civilians. Prosecutors will argue that he had the motivation and means to act on his beliefs. But others have suggested that perhaps the FBI, as Glenn Greenwald wrote in Salon, "found some very young, impressionable, disaffected, hapless, aimless, inept loner; created a plot it then persuaded/manipulated/entrapped him to join, essentially turning him into a terrorist; and then patted itself on the back." The disaffected loner is a frequent presence in jihadi Internet forums. Whether they themselves are dangers or are only dangerous when enticed to be by law enforcement is an unanswerable question.

Two years ago, Kohlmann testified in a case that many American Islamic leaders have called a clear instance of government entrapment. The investigation began when a group of young men who lived in and around Cherry Hill, New Jersey, brought a video to a nearby Circuit City to be transferred to DVD. The footage included the men shooting weapons and shouting *"Allahu akbar"* (God is great) in the Pocono Mountains. The clerk reported them to the local police, and the FBI subsequently dispatched two informants.

According to prosecutors, only one of the defendants spoke freely with the informant about his desire to join jihad and strike at Americans. He discussed various scenarios for attacks, and he took a drive with the informant to "case" Fort Dix. Three other men played paintball, shot guns, and tried to buy automatic weapons from another FBI informant. A fifth provided a map of the Fort Dix grounds. Together, the group watched videos of attacks on Americans.

It was acknowledged, however, that one of the defendants

told an informant that it was forbidden by Islam to kill American soldiers in America and declared on tape that they would never engage in suicide missions. "We just talk. We know," another was recorded saying. A third refused an offer to buy grenade launchers. And the defendant who provided a map of Fort Dix to the FBI informant did so because the informant had asked for it—and afterward tried to report the informant to the police.

Spending all his time scanning the web for jihadist activity has supplied Kohlmann with a narrative and a worldview, as well as the confidence to ascribe motivations to the narrative's players. Often, when he is called as a witness at a conspiracy trial, Kohlmann is shown a series of videos, writings, and wiretapped conversations with an informant and asked to identify the people and groups referred to within them. The defendants may not have any connection to those named other than the fact that the names are mentioned in these materials. But even a neutral recitation of this material can present a very damning impression of a very dangerous person.

"What Kohlmann is brought in to do is to tell the jury that conduct that might look innocent in other contexts should be viewed with alarm because of the associations a defendant has," says Vladeck. "It's a gray area he's working in here, because it walks a very fine line between prohibiting actual conduct and prohibiting associations, which is unconstitutional." There is, of course, a legitimate purpose to the use of experts in terrorism prosecutions. Kohlmann's virtually encyclopedic knowledge of names and dates and the broad narrative of jihad helps a jury to put a story in context.

But he is also used by prosecutors for another purpose: to keep the jury's attention fixed on their fears about the global conspiracy to murder Americans.

In the Fort Dix case, Kohlmann's "forensic analysis" of the defendants' hard drives concluded that the videos he found there "would be quite useful if you were planning a homegrown act of terrorism." He noted that three of the videos have been present on the hard drive of nearly every case he's worked on. "They are some of Al Qaeda's best work," he testified. At the end of his testimony, he was asked to reach a conclusion as to whether the materials were consistent with people conspiring to commit a violent act. He replied that they suggested "a clear, considered, and present danger to the community." The jury convicted the men of conspiracy charges, resulting in four life sentences and one sentence of thirty-three years.

"The great problem with these cases," says Vladeck, "is not that we can know that these defendants are innocent. Some of these conspirators probably are up to no good. But one quickly loses faith that we are drawing the right kinds of distinctions in every case." Magnus Ranstorp, the research director of the Center for Asymmetric Threat Studies at the Swedish National Defence College and a widely recognized authority on terrorism, believes that Kohlmann's conclusions rest on the most elementary social-scientific error: While it might be true that all self-radicalized terrorists watch jihadi videos, it does not follow that all people who watch jihadi videos become self-radicalized terrorists. "I think no serious academic would ever testify in such a cavalier fashion with such generalizations and quite frankly mumbo-jumbo-style analysis," he says. "It takes about thirty seconds to spot that Kohlmann produces junk science in court."

Kohlmann acknowledges that there are problems surrounding some of the cases at which he has testified but insists that prosecutors are doing the best they can, given the constraints they face. "I don't believe that there is any kind of deliberate malfeasance in these cases. Has every informant been perfect? No. Have I been involved in selecting those informants? No. Have the U.S. attorneys been entirely thrilled with all of them? No. But recruiting informants is not necessarily that easy. It's not a perfect system, but I'm pretty confident that I haven't been responsible for putting any innocent people behind bars."

Sometimes you glimpse in Kohlmann's eyes an unappeasable weariness. Maybe it's all the dark things he's been staring at for so many years, or maybe it's just a bad case of eyestrain. When I meet him in the MSNBC studio at 30 Rockefeller Plaza one morning, he has just returned from the doctor on account of his persistent migraines. He has already appeared on *Morning Joe* and is now back to prepare for a segment of *MSNBC Live*. Within minutes, he is talking to me about the intricacies of global jihad.

"Remember the name Abu Kandahar al-Zarqawi. You'll be hearing that name again," Kohlmann says, speaking over his shoulder as the tech straps on his mike. "He's lining up to be the next Humam al-Balawi. You know when you throw up a water balloon and can see where it's going to land? You can see where this one is going to land."

Earlier this year, Kohlmann's mood was lifted when a letter addressed to him was posted on an online forum. He sent the link in a mass email titled "Ansar Al-Mujahideen Online Forum Members Are Pissed at Me." But the excitement of tracking the terrorists through cyberspace is now dampened by the controversy he confronts at every trial. "It's not pleasant, when you work very hard at something and not only are your motives questioned but your knowledge, your experience, your credentials—everything you have built is questioned."

Kohlmann's primary assistant, who does most of his Arabic translation, is a gregarious, sweet-natured Jordanian grad student named Laith Alkhouri whom he found on Craigslist a year ago. He was hired as an intern but has grown into a close collaborator, watching the message boards with his boss and producing the PDFs that Kohlmann posts to his website, flashpoint-intel.com.

Kohlmann and Alkhouri have an easy, affectionate rapport. "I showed my mom the website to see my name on it, and she was like, 'You are going to scare me,'" says Alkhouri. "She said, 'I didn't know that this is what you do.' And she doesn't know half of what I do, really."

The job has become an all-consuming, twenty-four-hour-a-day passion for the two of them. "I prefer to work with people who have native language abilities, but more importantly, people who can grasp this," says Kohlmann. "It's very difficult to find people like that. Laith is one of the very few people who I've managed to identify who has the linguistic and cultural background to begin with and can also learn the technical aspect. But Laith now knows this stuff like I do."

Alkhouri chimes in: "No, you're the master. I'm not in the same category."

They hesitate, look at each other for a moment and then at me, slightly flustered, but then also proud.

One senses that Alkhouri renews for Kohlmann the spark of excitement he must have felt dipping into this shadowy netherworld for the first time, back in 1998, before anyone had heard of Al-Qaeda, when Kohlmann was among the first Americans peering through his Netscape browser at the metastasizing threat that would come to dominate the first decade of the twenty-first century. One wonders what cost Alkhouri will end up having to pay for that excitement and who else will end up sharing in the payment of it. "I could be the one to catch Bin Laden," says Alkhouri. "I know that's big talk! But if I just find the right message that could lead somewhere . . ."

New York Magazine, 2010

# 7

## ON FRANCIS FUKUYAMA

**THE FIRST VOLUME** of Francis Fukuyama's history of political development has been one of only a handful of books by a foreigner to make a profit in China. As Fukuyama explains when we meet near his home in Palo Alto, California, foreign books in China are usually pirated. But *The Origins of Political Order*, which narrates the emergence and growth of the state "From Prehuman Times to the French Revolution," engages respectfully with Chinese history and culture, and features an overarching version of national history that the Chinese themselves no longer teach or learn. Enough of his account of the country's enormous historic strengths and equally enormous historic weaknesses survived the censor's scalpel to make the work valuable to the Chinese reading public.

Fukuyama goes on to say that a friend in Beijing had learned that the Communist Party would translate that book's recently published companion volume, *Political Order and Political Decay,* for publication in a private edition for its senior leadership. "They take the analysis seriously," he said. The two volumes set out to compare and contrast the progression of various societies across time, in pursuit of a goal he calls "Getting to Denmark." The proverbial Denmark, like the actual state, is a robust liberal democracy with an effective state constrained by the rule of law—a package "so powerful, legitimate, and favorable to economic growth that it became a model to be applied throughout the world."

As he describes his reception in China, Fukuyama beams with pride that the authorities regard him as sufficiently impartial to take notice of, especially as he is perhaps the person most closely identified with the espousal of the victory of Western liberal democracy over all its ideological competitors. Fukuyama became an unlikely intellectual celebrity back in 1989 when he declared that the defeat of the USSR in the cold war represented not "the passing of a particular period of postwar history, but the end of history as such: that is, the end point of mankind's ideological evolution and the universalization of western liberal democracy as the final form of human government." To have written a book twenty-five years later that the Communist Party elite in Beijing feels compelled to make compulsory reading is a feat plainly gratifying to its author and ensures that his stern and chastening message will have been received by at least one of the audiences to whom it is addressed.

His book makes clear the fundamental debility of a political system lacking upward accountability, as the still nominally communist Chinese system does. But it also emphasizes the dangers of the improper sequencing of different elements of political development: too much rule of law too soon can constrain the development of an effective state, as happened in India; electoral democracy introduced in the absence of an autonomous administrative bureaucracy can lead to clientelism and pervasive corruption, as happened in Greece. Even the societies in which a proper balance of democracy, rule of law, and an effective state has been struck in the past are susceptible to political decay when rent-seeking extractive elite coalitions capture the state, as has happened in the United States. The failure of democratic institutions to function properly can delegitimize democracy itself and lead to authoritarian reaction, as happened in the former Soviet Union.

"They understand that their system needs fundamental political reform," Fukuyama says of the Chinese. "But they don't know how far they can go. They won't do what Gorbachev did, which was take the lid off and see what happens. But whether it will be possible to spread a rule of law to constrain state power at a pace that will satisfy the growing demands of the rising middle class is also unclear. There are 300 to 400 million Chinese in the middle class; that number will rise to 600 million in a decade. I had a debate a few years ago with an apologist for the regime. I pointed out that in many regions of the world when you develop a sufficiently large middle class, the pressure for increased political participation becomes irresistible. And the big question for China is whether there will be a point at which its people will push for greater participation, and he said: 'No, we're just culturally different.'"

It was, in effect, a rehash of the old "Asian values" argument concerning the hierarchical and deferential social ethic that goes by the name of Confucianism in east Asia—allegedly the reason that Asians lacked the impulse to individual self-assertion that resulted in the demand for self-government in other parts of the world. The democratic transitions in South Korea and Indonesia put an end to that argument decades ago, Fukuyama says, just as the Arab spring debunked a parallel claim regarding Arabs. This is the part of Fukuyama's argument about the end of history that he still stands behind without reservation or qualification—the Hegelian philosophical anthropology that saw history as the working out of the struggle between masters and slaves for recognition. "I really believe that the desire for recognition of one's dignity and worth is a human characteristic. You can see manifestations of this in all aspects of human behavior cross-culturally and through time."

The relevant historical analogue for the Chinese rulers, Fukuyama says, is probably Prussia under a series of enlightened monarchs, which allowed a rule of law to spread gradually without extending democratic participation to the people. But, of course, Germany came to the "end of history" after initiating and fighting two of the most brutal wars the world had ever seen.

Would the next rising power be able to control the titanic energies of its people and manage a transition that avoids the blood-letting Europeans had to endure? *Political Order and Political Decay* emphasizes the enormous difficulty of implanting democratic political institutions in places where the state has collapsed, or where it never really took root in the first place. For Fukuyama, the great challenge of state-building is creating and sustaining an institution of collective rule that cuts against the grain of human nature: we are designed to favor friends and family, and a patrimonial tribal order is "hard-wired," he argues, into our neural circuitry.

Though the right set of institutions can allow us to override these instincts, we naturally revert to them whenever political order breaks down. The first volume of his book recounts the expedients to which the first modern states resorted to overcome tribalism—it discusses the eunuchs who administered the Chinese state, the kidnapped Christian slaves who ran the Egyptian state—and the historical accidents that allowed state, society, and rule of law to reach an equilibrium favorable to modern political order in Western Europe. The second volume demonstrates how vulnerable even the best-developed modern state apparatus is to "repatrimonialization." Both volumes emphasize that the state is an institution that feeds on war, one whose national stability has often been buttressed by ethnic cleansing; and that the European Union after 1945, for instance, was built atop a pile of mass graves.

In some ways, Fukuyama says, he has been "trapped" by the ideological cul-de-sac in which his claims regarding the "end of history" have placed him. Though he still stands behind the assertion that liberal democracy is the eventual destination of history, he has qualified his argument and narrowed the scope of his ideological triumphalism, postponing the arrival of liberal democracy to the indefinite "long run." He would not, he tells me, use the same heightened rhetoric today that he used in 1989 to describe what he now calls a "historically contingent demand for greater political participation" that ensues as people become more prosperous and educated.

Fukuyama's career as a public intellectual began with an essay that promised to distinguish between "what is essential and what is contingent or accidental in world history." His own career, as he makes clear to me, was almost entirely a series of accidents. He took up ancient Greek under the influence of his charismatic freshman year teacher Allan Bloom, who inculcated him into the ideas of the émigré German philosopher Leo Strauss, and to a network of aspiring young intellectuals that included men who would figure prominently in his later career, Paul Wolfowitz and I. Lewis "Scooter" Libby. There was a detour into the modish French philosophers of the day, as part of which he made a pilgrimage to Paris (where he also wrote a novel) to study with Jacques Derrida, Jacques Lacan, and Roland Barthes. But he soon concluded, while enduring an interminable session in which Barthes would riff, pun, and free-associate over random sequences of words pulled from the dictionary, that "this was total bullshit, and why was I wasting my time doing it?"

He applied to Harvard's Kennedy School of Government to study national security. While the French poststructuralists and their epigones would go on to dominate American literature departments in the 1980s, his new cohort at the Kennedy School would populate the State Department and Pentagon. And in a remarkable turn of events, Fukuyama's old mentor Bloom would become a bestselling intellectual celebrity with *The Closing of the American Mind*, two years before Fukuyama's own ascent to global fame.

**"THE END OF HISTORY?"** began as something of a recondite joke. Fukuyama was at the time a midlevel figure in the Reagan State Department witnessing the rapid unraveling of the Soviet mystique. "I remember there was a moment when

Gorbachev said that the essence of communism was competition, and that's when I picked up the phone, called my friend and said, 'If he's saying that, then it's the end of history.'" Fukuyama is careful to point out that the coinage was not of his own making, but instead that of a Russian émigré professor named Alexander Kojève whose seminars on Hegel influenced postwar French existentialism.

But the triumphal eulogist of America at its world historical apogee never fell victim to the crude simplification of his own argument to which his neoconservative friends fell—and which his own rhetoric had done so much to invite. As he would later write in a 2006 book repudiating the neoconservativism of his youth, the misreading of the events of 1989 led directly to the calamities of the early 21st century that, in his view, have forever discredited the neocon approach to the world. "There was a fundamental misreading of that event and an ensuing belief that if America just did what Reagan had done, and stood firm, and boosted military spending, and used American hard power to stand up to the bad people of the world, we could expect the same moral collapse of our enemies in all instances." Fukuyama continues to credit Bloom and Strauss with broadening his intellectual horizons, but the adventure the adherents of those neocon thinkers embarked on, culminating in armed intervention in Baghdad, was, Fukuyama says, a bloody fiasco. "I don't know how they can live with the consequences of their actions."

Fukuyama has always been an intellectual comfortable with his proximity to power, conceiving of his role as offering guidance to the organs of the American national security state, starting with his first job at the RAND Corporation in the late 1970s. He has never indulged the romance of the adversary intellectual who sees the working of that system as irremediably corrupted. He showed me the cover of a recent issue of *Foreign Affairs* carrying an excerpt from *Political Order and Political Decay* whose headline announces "America in Decay," and indicated his discomfort with broadcasting a message that would give comfort to America's geopolitical adversaries.

It is one index of the state of American politics when a man of such impeccably centrist instincts feels impelled to assert, as Fukuyama has done, that the United States has become an oligarchy, and to lament the absence of a left-wing popular movement able to check the excesses of that oligarchy. He insists that he was right in the 1970s and 1980s to oppose the expansion of the welfare state, and to support the muscular use of American power around the globe during a time of retrenchment. But the pendulum has swung far in the other direction. "What I don't understand is my friends on the right who *don't* think it's necessary to rethink their ideas in light of subsequent events."

"I think where I've had my biggest and most positive audience is in recently democratized countries—Ukraine, Poland, Burma, and Indonesia," he says. "In places like that, I'm still a rock star. In places like that, the End of History writings allowed people to see themselves as a broad historical movement. It wasn't just their local little disputes; there were deeper principles involved. And to be able to go to those places and tell them that they are on the right side of history with regard to political change—to this day I'm touched by it. To be able to go to Kiev and tell people there that democracy still remains the wave of the future—it's in those moments that I feel most fully that I've made and am making a lasting contribution."

*The Guardian, 2014*

# PART III

## 8

---

# INSIDE THE BOX

**I KNEW ABOUT BRITNEY SPEARS** a few months before the rest of the world. What I mean by this is that I was a viewer of The Box in 1998. You could call into The Box to request a video, and the idea was that at some interval after you had made your call, the video you had requested would appear. I sometimes thought about doing this, but the logistics of it seemed daunting to me, and I could never muster the nerve. Instead, I was content to watch the videos that others had chosen, which were not the videos I would have chosen. To judge by the videos that did play—and there seemed no difference between this pseudodemocracy and the usual kind of preprogrammed channel, since the same handful of videos rotated with numbing regularity—The Box catered to an "urban" demographic underserved by MTV, which was then in a transitional phase of its existence, long past the heroic days when it featured gender-bending synth-pop from limp-wristed limeys with a perpetual sob in their voice, and just at the beginning of Carson Daly's brazen ascent at *Total Request Live* (*TRL*).

The Box played the trashiest videos by the trashiest acts with the lowest production values. And many of these videos showed a lot of skin, which made them an indispensable resource to young men caught in the New Jersey suburbs. Back then, in the days of dial-up Internet access (and it may be hard for our younger readers to conceive of this), it was hard to find things to masturbate to if you weren't ready to admit—as mostly people weren't, back then—that you were a disgusting pervert willing to spend money to see women treated like objects in front of a camera.

If you had one of the old cable boxes, you could press channels 3, 5, and 7 simultaneously and get a flickering, distorted look at the Playboy Channel. Sometimes the screen resembled a gold mosaic bearing the faint outlines of an image; other times a chaos of harsh colors in scrambled flux. Occasionally, it would resolve into a clear image, though only for a few seconds at a time. You would see a breast surging in slow motion as it passed through a sprinkler, brushed by the water's prismatic spray, or cutoff jean shorts shucked off onto a hay bale. Or a car wash would degenerate into a naked sudsy free-for-all. Though you could not hear, you could imagine the various soundtracks—the perfunctory fiddle and banjo accompanied with the airless Syndrum beat; the warthog growl and squeal of a neon-pink B.C. Rich, as the guy with the black-painted fingernails eased off the whammy bar. Time was short: You had to be ready to respond to these inducements, to answer the call to solitary arousal.

If you wanted to see a picture of a penis penetrating a vagina, you had to venture out to a former warehouse space on the West Side Highway and pay $25 for a magazine that came hidden in a brown paper sleeve. You had to put yourself in the company of seedy characters bathed in blear light amid the all-pervading odor of ammonia. If this was your interest, you desired something known then as "hardcore" pornography, which was ostensibly against the law as recently as the early 1990s. It was a curious time to be trapped in the hormonal tempest of that period of life—between the Meese Commission's report on pornography, and the publication of Catharine MacKinnon's groundbreaking work on sexual harassment (and more than thirty years after the release of the Beatles' first LP)—when one of the consequences of sexual exploration was death from an incurable illness, and when Christian morality and radical feminism both inveighed against what the consumption of pornography was doing to the heart and soul and loins of a people.

We took these dire admonitions at least partially seriously, we earnest youth of America, because though we didn't really believe in any Christian creed, we believed that there was something inherently precious and singular in everyone (but particularly in ourselves) that deserved to be loved, something that was endlessly fragile and needful of protection. Even if we held the hysterical aspects of campus feminism at a remove, we believed that equality was the foundation of the true love that would express itself in an intimate, mutually fulfilling eroticism. That's what we thought back then.

My mood in those days was somnolent. I drove a 1989 Nissan Pulsar NX that my parents had bought me for $500. I was working as a reporter at a free weekly newspaper in East Brunswick, New Jersey, earning $15,482 a year and living in Milltown, New Jersey. I would drive down a peculiar strip of

Route 18 that looked like one of those long tracking shots that filmmakers rely on to establish a mise-en-scène of anonymity and cheapness—those garish colors attenuated by years of grime, those ghostly commercial icons suspended on massive pedestals projecting into the sky, and all those tons of polished metal darting around the off-ramps bearing their vulnerable human cargo. You grew accustomed to risking death at the jug-handled turn ramps that were unique to New Jersey highways. It felt like the end of the world.

The music I preferred on these excursions were hissy dubbed cassette tapes of Glenn Gould playing Bach in that bludgeoning, affectless style he invented, so remorseless in its inhuman power. The music, turned up all the way so as to be audible over the wide-open windows—the car had no air-conditioning—felt a little bit like purgatory, and a little bit like anesthesia, and most of all like the cold rapture of thought struggling to transcend its surroundings. I've never felt as alone as I did in that little box, the hot wind battering my face, cutting through those desolate stretches of big-box stores, passing through the newly built subdivisions that had sprung up on raw pastureland. But sometimes, when the music was high, and the sun was a hot smear at high noon, or you were hurtling down an empty stretch of road at night, you felt the immense power of the car you were driving to propel you beyond yourself and into . . . Jameson called it the hysterical sublime.

Those were the days when (if I wasn't watching The Box) I would work my way through the dense thickets of the pseudophilosophical jargon that proposed to name this condition in which I was living, to dignify it with a lofty vocabulary that radiated a paranoid dread that seemed to be the only feeling worth feeling back then, the only feeling that was real and alive. What was this malign historical stasis I was living through, that my own life seemed so helpless a product of, in which there was no fate beyond bored passivity in the face of capitalism's triumphal march?

When I first saw Britney Spears on The Box, in the fall of 1998, what I thought about was Britny Fox. Now, Britny Fox was a terrible hair metal band that had scored a hit earlier in the nineties with a song called "Girlschool." It featured a classroom full of Catholic schoolgirls gyrating to the beat in defiance of a stern teacher. They roll up their shirts to expose their abs, and muss their hair, but they don't go any further—there isn't anywhere further to go. Thus the video, which started off promisingly, reaches a narrative impasse, and the women just keep swaying around in the classroom for the rest of the song.

But that was a sexist video by a horrible hair metal band that exploited women. Britney Spears was something else— an inflection point in the culture. *TRL*'s arrival in Times Square was an important signpost in that neighborhood's new identity. Giuliani's quality-of-life police ran out the junkies and the prostitutes. Disney remade the square as a gleaming, candy-colored monument to anodyne, family-friendly, corporate-sponsored mass entertainment. Britney, the former Mouseketeer, literally straddled the divide between Times Square's old and new identities. It was a further elaboration of the "winner take all system" that still obtained in the world of 1998, whereby all the money that might once have supported an ecosystem of joke-tellers in the Catskills was sitting in Jay Leno's pocket. Instead of an army of diseased whores, there would be one perfectly airbrushed youth whom the whole world would watch together.

Now, none of this became clear to me until the spring of 2001, when Pepsi ran an amazing ad in which Bob Dole is sitting alone in his bedroom, bathed in that eerie blue light cast by the TV screen, watching Britney Spears dance around singing an anthem of generational change that is also a paean to Pepsi. And this one-handed war hero and presidential aspirant who was, by that time, better known as a commercial spokesman for Viagra, is as engrossed by the image of the young Spears as any man who would like to have an erection but requires the help of cutting-age technology would be. His dog barks, and Dole says: "Down, Boy."

And there was something about this moment more eloquent, radical, and true than anything I had read in those candy-colored paperbacks. It was like a wild utopian novel condensed into a single, electric image: freedom, spontaneity, youth, and a sexuality that was boundless, innocent, and all-encompassing confronting age, authority, infirmity, limitation, subsuming and vanquishing it. Or it was like a dark dystopian satire folded into an instant: a man of power and authority prostituting himself to the seduction of a dream world concocted by corporate masters who feed out endlessly deferred dreams of power, success, and love in the name of fizzy, corn-syrupy water. The commercial did not merely suggest, but actually demonstrated in the most palpable way, that no man had the dignity to rise above this fate.

Most of all, it was a picture of the world as it was, it felt like the American present, and it felt like life. I went on

Amazon and liquidated what remained of those theory books while they still retained some value. It was the spring of 2001 and American prosperity was at its height. We had elected George W. Bush president, Britney Spears was the biggest pop star in the world, and I had finally acquired a broadband connection. I was ready for what was to come.

*n+1, 2009*

# 9

# ON READING THE SEX DIARIES

**SO THERE'S THIS IPHONE APP** called Grindr. It's a GPS-enabled social-networking service for gay men. It tells you how many feet away a possible hookup is standing. Each profile comes with a picture, a tagline, the relevant stats, and a declaration of interest. You scroll through a column of heads and torsos arranged in descending order of proximity, tapping on the ones that seem promising and chatting with the ones who want the same things you do. As you make your way through the city, the menu of men reshuffles, and the erotic terrain updates in real time.

Has the search for erotic gratification ever been so efficient? Until recently, being a cad or coquette took a lot of work: You needed to buy a little black book, and you had to go around filling it, and then you had to schedule your calls for a time when the target of your seduction was likely to be at home. The less self-assured daters in New York faced the sickening anxiety of the first phone call, or the cold approach in the bar. There were palliatives designed to help people cope—the newspaper personal ads, the paid dating services, the dirty videos and magazines—but they were generally understood to be the province of weirdos and losers.

No more. The social technologies that assist in dating and mating today are more than palliatives—they've changed the nature of the game. If the cold approach is more than you can deal with, put up a Craigslist ad, or join OkCupid, Manhunt, or Nerve. If the phone call makes you nervous, send a text message. And while you're at it, send a text message to a half-dozen other people with everyone's favorite late-night endearment: "where u at?" If nothing works out and you find yourself alone at home again, simply fire up XTube or YouPorn and choose from an endless variety of positions to help you reach a late-night climax.

Virtually everyone under the age of thirty has grown up with their sexuality digitally enhanced, and the rest of us are rapidly forgetting the world before we all were hooked into the same erotically charged network of instantaneously transmitted messages and images. This must be true across the country, but it seems particularly suited for a city as dense, morally libertine, and sexually spirited as New York. Part of the promise of this city has always been that there's another prospective partner a subway stop away, but not until recently could that partner interrupt your daily business with a cell-phone snapshot of their parted thighs. And of course, the same technology that makes it easier to score also makes the sexual boast or confession easily transmissible to millions of other people.

Every Monday since April 2007, this magazine has posted on its Daily Intel blog a seven-day diary of an anonymous New Yorker's sex life. It began as an experiment intended to entertain the bored at work, but the candor of the Diarists soon attracted an outsize and devout following. Since October 2007, they have been joined by a rambunctious cacophony of commenters as obsessive on the subject of sex as the Diarists themselves. They criticize, malign, offer support and tips, and digress into arguments about everyone else's sex lives, as well as their own. The Diaries are often flooded with over 100 comments within 24 hours. Two months ago, the comments on one diary were closed down at 895.

Over the course of the Sex Diaries' 132-week run, we have seen the city through the eyes of cuckolds and cheaters, sluts and prudes, victimizers and victims, starry-eyed lovers and detached pleasure seekers. We have followed aging women on dismal Craigslist dates, lonely gay men in pursuit of ostensibly curious straight guys, happily polyamorous couples, and codependent serial monogamists. We've watched some Diarists terrified of succumbing to their feelings and others unable to feel much of anything at all. We've watched a black man fly to meet a white couple at a TGI Fridays in the Midwest and have sex with the wife as the husband watched.

The Diaries can be arousing, a little. But in aggregate, they wound up doing something more interesting: They cracked open a window into the changing structure, rhythm, and rhetoric of sex in New York. The Diarists are a self-selecting group, of course: bizarrely oversharing New Yorkers motivated by the impulse to brag or, as often, the urge to fling their terrible abjection in the face of the world. But as we watched them struggle with the peculiar hazards of mating in New York today (failing spectacularly, or succeeding all too well), we saw that their hassles were everyone's writ large, and their stories posed a question: Are the digital tools that make it easier to find sex compounding the confusion that accompanies it?

The editors of this magazine asked me to read all 800 pages of the Sex Diaries, and, using them as a source text, develop some kind of taxonomy of contemporary sexual anxieties. (Let others parse Chaucer, my role was that of exegete of "The Polyamorous Paralegal.") So that's what I've done. Herewith: ten things that seem to be making our playful, amorous youth crazy.

## 1. THE ANXIETY OF TOO MUCH CHOICE

A fact so readily apparent that it has escaped reflection: The cell phone has changed the nature of seduction. One carries in one's pocket, wherever one goes, the means of doing something other than what one is presently doing, or being with someone other than the person one is with. Take this excerpt from a thirty-one-year-old straight male Diarist ("The Transportation Coordinator Seeing Three Partners") living on the Upper West Side:

> 12:32 p.m. I get three texts. One from each girl. E wants oral sex and tells me she loves me. A wants to go to a concert in Central Park. Y still wants to cook. This simultaneously excites me—three women want me!— and makes me feel odd.

This is a distinct shift in the way we experience the world, introducing the nagging urge to make each thing we do the single most satisfying thing we could possibly be doing at any moment. In the face of this enormous pressure, many of the Diarists stay home and masturbate.

## 2. THE ANXIETY OF MAKING THE WRONG CHOICE

A Diarist with any game at all has unlimited opportunity. A few find this enjoyable and are up to the task: Identify the single best sexual partner available, or at least the person most amenable to their requirements at the moment. They use their cell phone to disaggregate, slice up, and repackage their emotional and physical needs, servicing each with a different partner, and hoping to come out ahead. This can get complicated quickly, however, and can lead to uneasy situations.

An inordinate number of Diarists find themselves at the brink of enjoying one sexual experience, only to receive a phone call or text from another potential suitor. They become a slave to their compulsion and indecision. Consider these snippets in a week of one Diarist, who is deeply conflicted between Pseudo and Ex:

> *2:55 p.m. Pseudo G-chats me. Looks like he might be interested in hanging out tonight after all.*
>
> *9:30 p.m. Meet up with Ex and friends at bar. Text Pseudo to see if he's up for doing anything.*
>
> *2:20 a.m. At a bar with Pseudo and other friends. Ex drunk-texts me: "Wanna fuck?"*
>
> *3:17 a.m. Half-bottle of wine plus mucho beer plus a few rounds of shots leads to me texting Pseudo, "Let's get out of here and go back to my place."*

*3:18 a.m. Pseudo texts back, "I don't feel like dealing with you."*

*11:45 p.m. At a bar with Pseudo. Ex drunk-texts me.*

*1:30 p.m. Ex calls and wakes me up. Says he needs to talk in person.*

*7:49 p.m. Text Pseudo and tell him about convo with Ex. Pseudo replies that he's sorry, he hopes I end up getting what I want. What the hell does that mean? I have no idea what I want, clearly.*

This compulsive toggling between options winds up inflicting the very damage it was designed to protect against.

### 3. THE ANXIETY OF NOT BEING CHOSEN

Among active Diarists, the worry that they will make the wrong choice is surpassed by the fear that they might find themselves without one. To guard against this disaster, everybody is on somebody's back burner, and everybody has a back burner of their own, which they maintain through open-ended texts, sporadic Facebook messages, Gchats, IM's, and terse emails. The Diarists appear to do this regardless of whether or not they are in a committed, or even a contractually sealed, relationship.

*12:22 a.m. Tell him I want him. Clothes off, oral sex given and received.*

*12:45 a.m. IM sound from my computer. I'm currently busy, but I have a feeling who it is at this hour. Continue deliciously illicit activities which turn into both intercourse and mutual masturbation.*

> *1:50 a.m. After we finish, check IM. I was spot-on; it*
> *is Mr. 34. And we all know what 2 a.m. IM's mean.*

Sometimes being relegated to the back burner is a sign of uninterest: the late-night booty call, the option of last resort. As often, it is a place to confine anyone who might become emotionally dangerous. The back burner is a confusing, destabilizing, and exhausting place to be, and yet none of the Diarists—even ones who appear sexually sated—appear to view it as anything but a fact of life. It is clearly less terrifying than the alternative, which is to not be on anyone's.

### 4. THE ANXIETY OF APPEARING OVERLY ENTHUSIASTIC

The back burner is a game, and while the Diarists have various ideas about what constitutes winning, they all agree on how you lose: by betraying a level of emotional enthusiasm unmatched by the other party. Everyone's afraid disarmament won't be mutual.

To disarm unilaterally is a strategic error on so many levels—it commits you to a degree of openness you might not be able to maintain, and it exposes vulnerabilities that your counterparty might not be able to resist exploiting. It signals desperation, clinginess, high-maintenance. Most of all, it risks exposing the fond hope, better kept to oneself, that one yearns to leave behind the serial fuck buddies, friends with benefits, and other back-burner relationships to which one had, at some significant expenditure of effort, inured oneself.

The goal of any Diarist playing the game, therefore, is to withhold one's own expectations until one understands what is expected by the other party. These negotiations require supreme discipline. If you betray the wrong kind of avidity at the wrong moment, your counterparty will not hesitate to pitch you into the shark tank:

> *3:30 a.m. I text Mike. . .that I had a good time and would really like to hang out. Ten minutes later he texts me back saying the he would "be down" for hanging out and that we should do it on a weeknight when things aren't crazy with the parties. I text him back saying he is confusing. He asks how. I felt daring and told him because I can never tell what he wants from me. I haven't heard from him since.*

The Diaries are filled with these kinds of casualties and near misses. ("I love this man," thinks one Diarist mid-coitus. "Mental anxiety attack when I realize I almost said this out loud.") The commenters have no sympathy for these emotional miscalculations. This, by contrast, from one of the most well-received Diaries ("The TV Producer Who Knows Everyone") that ever ran:

> *3 p.m. Already received two texts and countless Facebook IM's from the Brit. Am slowly starting to realize I have a Stage Five Clinger on my hands. He asks me to hang out again this coming Sunday. I do not respond.*

This Diary contained all of the elements that commenters favored: lots of action, multiple partners, emotional fickleness, bad judgment brashly flaunted, and tasty little morsels of private pain offered up in a drolly ingratiating tone.

## 5. THE ANXIETY OF APPEARING DELUSIONAL

The quality in a Sex Diary most admired by commenters is the kind of confidence (or masochism) that allows for ruthless candor. The commenters, it should be said, are a community unto themselves: part intimate support group, part vengeful gathering of Maoist Red Guards. Friends and underminers both, they make it clear that they are not just looking for masturbation material. They celebrate Diarists who exhibit the virtue of self-knowledge, and descend on those oblivious to their own weakness.

The Diarists seemed to recognize this, and over the years the journals have become increasingly reflective, with observational riffs and little bits of self-analysis. One Diarist calls herself "the most emotionally detached woman in the history of New York." "I should probably be in therapy," says another Diarist, "but instead I'm just hedonistic, and don't let anyone get close. I know it's all a power play."

These are statements of psychological awareness, but they are also performances. They mask a deeper fear: that one might not be in complete control of one's appearance. The Diarists cannot bear being judged without having let us know they have properly anticipated it.

## 6. THE ANXIETY OF APPEARING OVERLY SINCERE

Though the Diarists flaunt their emotional honesty, much of what they confess to concerns their terror of losing control. And there is no more efficient way to relinquish control than a sincere avowal of emotion.

The Diarists with the most active auctions use cutesy neologisms to assign categories to the multitude confronting them. One Diarist has three prospects: "the Ex-Boyfriend's Friend (XBFF), the Art Director, and potentially the Love of My Life." She's hoping of the XBFF that "we can maybe talk about a possible long-distance pseudo-relationship." (And she has been avoiding calling the potential LOML.) Another sends a cell-phone pic of her cleavage to "Band Dude" on day two of her Diary, but later that week finds herself in bed with the "Pseudo-Ex."

The funny little names make for easy reading—they protect identities, and help us readers keep up with the narrative convolutions. But they also perform an important conceptual labor, subtly ironizing the ones about whom one might conceivably have feelings and neatly dismissing those labeled as a means to an end. There is a certain pride in understanding the limits of a transaction, and installing oneself in the safe position of narrator. This is particularly true for the female Diarists eager to portray themselves just as capable of using others as any man.

You could argue that this playing-to-the-audience is a product of unique circumstances—the Sex Diaries are written for a readership, of course—but postgame narration and color commentary, like rigorous self-analysis, are a constant element of New York mating. Sometimes it feels like the principal reason we have friends.

## 7. THE ANXIETY OF APPEARING PRUDISH

The Diarists are eager to show themselves to have conquered modesty—as if anyone is still insisting they be modest. This is particularly true of the young women—and the Diaries are full of them—who operate at the weird place where male pornographic fantasies and their own fantasies of self-empowered pleasure converge:

> *11:39 p.m. Dance with a couple of my girlfriends. We spot some cute guys in the corner checking us out. Decide to give the guys a show and lock lips with one another. Watch guys' jaws drop to the floor.*

As for pornography, it plays a role in an extraordinary number of Diaries. Still, few Diarists of either sex are willing to betray any discomfort with it, per se. ("See, I have no issue with porn," one Diarist assures us when discussing his friend's enormous collection.) Instead they worry about everything *related* to porn. Its price, for instance. Or a partner's overindulgence. Occasionally, they do fear that the consumption of it may be wearing them out. This, it seems, is incontestable. The experiences of the lonely and the overstimulated by too much sex converge in weirdly affecting moments of intimacy. Picture the montage—a series of apartments in the soft, gray light of dawn:

> *10 p.m. Contemplate masturbating, pass out before I can summon the strength to find my vibrator.*
>
> *3:01 a.m. Attempt to masturbate. Pass out with the vibrator still going.*
>
> *3:30 a.m. Wake up with porn on my laptop and cock in hand. I guess I was really tired.*

## 8. INTERNET—ENABLED AGORAPHOBIA

For some Diarists, online dating has become not just a supplement to their social lives but a replacement for it. They prefer to game out all the angles of each prospective seduction ahead of time—to "control the environment and the message," as one Diarist puts it—and regard the social world itself as "asinine bullshit/social Kabuki."

The most practiced online daters have mastered the paradoxical etiquette of meeting strangers online and attaining swift mutual satisfaction:

> *11 a.m. I come across an ad from a sincere-looking South Asian fellow and respond. The fellow responds with a number. I call and we agree to hook up for drinks.*
> *6:17 p.m. The fellow and I do a 69.*

Simple. But a certain callousness toward the merchandise is an unavoidable side effect of entering a marketplace as both buyer and seller. If any of the Diarists have felt the sting of disappointment in finding an Internet correspondence go dead, they are immune to it now. They refer to online solicitations as if they were bidders on eBay, and browse potential options without the slightest titillation:

> *2:30 p.m. Cruise Manhunt, Craigslist, and Adam4Adam in a desultory manner. I'm not really horny. It's kinda like picking up takeout menus from neighborhood restaurants. I just want to know what's available.*

The loneliest Diarists, seeking a respite from their loneliness, often find people even lonelier than themselves:

> *1 p.m. Kick off my weekly Sunday-afternoon tradition: "Find Steve on Craigslist." Steve is a disgusting person I slept with back in April, who attributed my lack of an orgasm to his use of a hair-replacement product. Every Sunday, sure as the rising sun, he posts an ad where he comments about the weather and requests a "beautiful companion" to go to the beach/take a walk in the park/get a coffee/see a movie. He sickens me.*

### 9. SEPARATION ANXIETY

Collecting all of your friends onto a single page, as all social-networking sites do, alters the way you think about experiences. Formerly, you met people, did things with them, and selected a handful to carry forward into later stages of life. Life was a linear sequence of relationships that began and ended.

But just as Facebook has become an instrument for meeting and seducing new people, it is now also an archive of people you had once seduced or been seduced by:

> *2:30 p.m. Trying to put off my homework even more, I scan through my Facebook account, my BlackBerry, and my in-box trying to think if I am friends with any guys who I haven't hooked up with already. Zilch.*

And just as the new technologies keep reminding us of the existence of these old relationships, so they make the temptation to relationship recidivism irresistible to many of the Diarists. It seems as if half of the Diarists are either texting or being texted by old flames:

> *10:30 p.m. He has not called me back, I'm frustrated. Though we broke up a year ago, we usually see each other quite often; however it's not clear if he is my boyfriend once again. I'm still in love with him. . . . Don't want to pressure him, because it's the reason we broke up in the first place. I begin to think, What do I do to keep him interested and wanting only me?*

Maintaining enough distance to permit a decisive break now requires more discipline than many people can muster, and a familiar category of relationship has become more widespread: those that one can never wholly embrace, but never finally refuse. This is wireless codependency, and the recovery movement potent enough to cure it (without insisting that its members unplug from the grid) has yet to come into being.

## 10. THE ANXIETY OF BEING UNABLE TO LOVE

And yet perhaps the most surprising psychological attribute of the Diarists, despite weeks upon weeks of guarding their vulnerabilities from the brutality of the marketplace, is their romanticism. True love! Who could say these words in public without acute embarrassment? It is nonetheless something that the Diarists keep referencing, despite the impression they convey that it is an ever-receding ideal. It's an odd, negative sort of tribute—a vague longing for something all but lost, but perhaps worth clinging to nonetheless.

*10 p.m. I want to love her. And I should. I just, well, don't. She's the best girlfriend anyone could ever hope to have. I wish that were enough to love her.*

Reading the Sex Diaries all in one enormous gulp, as I have, caused me to surf on the edge of a terrible vertigo as I thought of the many wounds I had myself endured and inflicted during my brief career as a person with a New York City sex life. I had a thought analogous to the one I often have about cars: How is it that we hurtle around the country in these enormous steel boxes and ever survive? And yet people do, sometimes even in the Sex Diaries.

You would have to have read 800 printed pages of them to feel about the following Diary the same way that I did. There was nothing special about it—just an ordinary young man earnestly seeking a happy ending—and it is surely because I endured so much of the heartbreak written into this sprawling document that I make no apologies for the pleasure I took in it, or in disclosing that the somewhat sappy narrative climax contained therein brought me—in my own high esteem, as disenchanted a reader as any alive today—to tears in the reading room of the New York Public Library:

*DAY SEVEN*

*11:15 a.m. Co-worker makes comment that I am glowing. I smile, knowing it's because of new boyfriend. 3 p.m. I write note to Ex explaining how I thought he should know that I am really happy and dating an amazing guy. It finally feels like some closure. 7 p.m. My head is in the clouds, and I forget to bring my sneakers to my dodgeball game. Still we are able to win one game. I catch game-winning ball! 9:35 p.m. Guy from league hits on me. I happily deny him: "Sorry, I just met an amazing guy, and I think I'm in love!" I smile, feeling really good about telling anyone and everybody about how happy I am and how wonderful he is. I cannot wait for our date tomorrow!*

*New York Magazine, 2009*

# 10

# GAME THEORY

THE "SEDUCTION COMMUNITY"—most insidious of oxymorons—grew up on message boards and newsgroups when the Internet was still a place of social exile. The early adopters were people prepared to start life anew—that is, losers. As in recovery movements, acknowledging the problem was the first step.

These were hard-up men perplexed by women and determined to figure them out, as they had figured out the algorithms of the computer programs they wrote, or the patterns and strategies they mastered to make it through the video games they played. They were nerds who had been pushed around by jocks and made envious of cool guys all their lives. There were things that cool guys did, innocently, as a function of their social programming, that made them cool. The losers were going to study their behavior, and they were going to start replicating it. And once they were done with the process of breaking down what the successful behaviors were and why they worked, and once they were done rewiring their own brains (which are far more plastic, the neurologists tell us, than we have ever imagined), they would find they could react in new ways to the old, scary stimuli they got from women—ways even more effective than those of their persecutors. In fact, because they were taking a methodical approach to what others did only by instinct, and because they had an analytic understanding of what others did in an unpremeditated way, they were going to be better at being cool guys than any truly cool guy could ever be.

They renamed each other, taking on talismanic handles, each of which declared a secret hope. Mystery. Extramask. Juggler. Playboy. Sin. Lovedrop. Matador. At sites like alt.seduction.fast.com, men from around the world posted detailed narrative accounts of their dates, soliciting, offering, and receiving critical dissection of every statement and gesture. The men volunteered their experiences as data in a vast scientific trial that no responsible researcher would ever attempt. You could even say that these men were engaged in a strange parody of the activities of the men of the Enlightenment, who used the printing press to diffuse a new attitude toward life that broke with the inherited traditions and dogmas of the past. It was a free and open exchange of ideas across international borders in which men distilled the chaos of experience into universal principles. Together they created a body of knowledge that was rational, pragmatic, purposive, and—above all—subject to the test of experiment.

By means of the collective efforts of hundreds of recovering AFCs (average frustrated chumps, in the literature) and aspiring PUAs (pickup artists), they were able to observe, tag, categorize, and devise a winning response to every twitch, flutter, or hesitation that a woman might offer in the progress, as their eventual leader Mystery would flatly put it, "from meet—to sex." If a subject looked back at all his successful sexual encounters, he would see that each and every one of them passed through a sequence of three stages. Mystery defined these as attraction, building comfort, and seduction. By detaching oneself from the welter of passions that afflict us in our everyday behaviors, one could arrive at a method to move through those stages, consciously and with maximum efficiency.

All of us who have tried and failed to break through to the opposite sex think about what works and what doesn't when it comes to the entirely unnatural sociability one must learn to master in a city full of strangers. The Internet created a new space to transform that blind empirical groping into what would become, in the hands of its most gifted practitioners, a positivistic system of human relations.

**WE HAVE A RECORD,** of sorts, of what the world of the pickup arts used to be like. Tom Cruise is the medium, in the role of Frank T. J. Mackey in *Magnolia*. Mackey opens his class by slowly flexing his biceps beneath a brightening spotlight on a darkened stage of a rented hotel conference room. Richard Strauss's *Also sprach Zarathustra* blasts through the speakers.

"*Respect* the cock!" Cruise shouts, to the answering cries and bellows, hoots and chanting, of his audience, "and"— with this he launches himself to the lip of the stage, revealing his chiseled face to the camera, kneeling with his arm outstretched in a gesture of embattled striving—"*tame* the cunt!"

His students are beefy rage-filled mooks in pleated Dockers. They work themselves into a frenzy at every cue, including the moment in Cruise's presentation when he feigns the act of intercourse—intercourse from behind—onstage. They learn how to, as the overhead projections tell them, "Fake Like You Are a Nice and Caring Guy." They are instructed to "Form a Tragedy," as a technique for earning sympathy, all in service of turning "Your 'Friend' into a 'Sperm Receptacle.' "

Cruise's portrayal was a cartoon that nonetheless captured something about the state of the pickup artists in their early days. The pioneering figure of the online seduction community was a man named Ross Jeffries; the music writer Neil Strauss, in his immersive account of the PUA world titled *The Game*, describes him as a "tall, skinny, porous-faced self-proclaimed nerd." Jeffries's early ebooks, which relied on a pseudohypnotic technique called neurolinguistic programming (which instructs its would-be practitioners to "seed" conversation with subtly hidden commands that will act on the subconscious of the recipient), were crudely written and full of sarcasm, resentment, and rage. They were distinguished by the typographical quirkiness, tonal crudeness, and brash salesmanship common to the work of autodidactic experts. In their desperate insistence and at least partial honesty, they are also strangely touching.

"There's no such *'thing'* as love. There's no such *'thing'* as passion. There's no such *'thing'* as attraction, or chemistry, or lust," Jeffries wrote in one of his early manuals.

I know, I know, you're saying. That's the problem . . . for most of you, most of the time, there's no such thing. There's just boredom, frustration, and playing with Mr.

Winky. But that's not what I'm talking about, so pay
close attention.

I'm not saying that people don't experience *states* of
'attraction' or 'chemistry' or 'lust.'

What I am saying is that these states are processes
that take place inside the human mind and body. Which
means that they are states that . . .

*CAN BE SUMMONED FORTH AND DIRECTED AT
WILL!!!*


**NEIL STRAUSS LEARNED** about this community just as it was
beginning to make its transition from being the obsession
of a few isolated weirdos to a flourishing commercial venture for many weirdos. He was handed a copy of one of the
first "Layguides" and ventured onto the message boards as a
reporter researching a story. It didn't take long for him to lose
his reportorial detachment. Soon he was stuffing $500 cash
into an envelope addressed to Mystery, a legendary figure on
the message boards who had coined many of the terms in the
PUA lexicon. Strauss overcomes the reader's skepticism with
the same élan with which he learned to "blast last-minute
resistance," conceding, with disarming candor, that it is "no
easy feat to sign up for a workshop dedicated to picking up
women. To do so is to acknowledge defeat, inferiority and
inadequacy. It is to finally admit to yourself that after all
these years of being sexually active (or at least sexually cog-
nizant) you have not grown up and figured it out."

By the time Strauss arrived on the scene, the pickup
artists had already begun to clean up their act. The docu-

ments they wrote were becoming more professional in their style and presentation, the theoretical framework had grown more sophisticated. The experts had begun to scrub away the resentment and raw misogyny adhering to the community's rhetoric. Accordingly, a new kind of student entered the scene: good-looking, successful, and competent men who were looking to make their sex lives less like gambling and more like shopping. These men had other aspects of their lives working; now they wanted to "solve" the woman problem.

Strauss was present at the first seminar, run by Mystery, at which students actually left the classroom to go "in field." Mystery began by explaining the basic structure of seduction—FMAC, for find, meet, attract, and close. He explained the power of the mysterious "neg," one of the great innovations of the seduction community. Strauss describes it thus:

> Neither compliment nor insult, a neg is something in between—an accidental insult or backhanded compliment. The purpose of the neg is to lower a woman's self-esteem while actively displaying a lack of interest in her—by telling her she has lipstick on her teeth, for example, or offering her a piece of gum after she speaks.

"I don't alienate ugly girls," Mystery explains. "I don't alienate guys. I only alienate the girls I want to fuck."

It was 2002. Armies of outlandishly dressed men (done up in accordance with "peacock theory") began appearing in bars around the country. "Did you see those two girls fighting outside?" they would ask their targets, delivering the same canned material time and time again. They would come in with their bodies at an angle and give the appearance of being ready to leave at any moment. "I can't stay long—I've got to get back to my friends," they would say, delivering the "false time constraint" that preempts any social discomfort their entrance into the "set" would generate. With their first entrance, they'd "buy the next thirty seconds," and with the story they told, they'd buy the next two minutes, while "demonstrating higher value" through precisely calibrated routines. "I need a quick female opinion on something," they'd begin, and then launch into a story. "Would you let your boyfriend keep a box of photos of his ex-girlfriend? Because my buddy . . ." They'd talk to the "obstacles" (the ugly girls surrounding the target) and the men in the set, conspicuously ignoring the target. When she began to clamor for their attention, they'd throw out a neg. "I like your nails. Are they real?" Strauss carried around, in his seduction kit, a large ball of lint that he would pick off a girl's sweater. (Strauss eventually received historical confirmation of the value of the neg when he learned that Warren Beatty would blow his nose and hand the crumpled tissue to a woman.) Then the men would reverse course, give the target an opportunity to demonstrate her higher value, and play push-pull, like dancing a string around for a cat to chase. Once you have reached the "hook point," when she stops wondering when you're going to leave and begins looking for ways to make you stay, then it's time to propose an "instant date"—"bounce" to another club, party, or diner, to embed the impression of familiarity. "Every location that you move with her in which she doesn't wind up raped and murdered by you," Mystery observes, "builds comfort." And when it comes down to last-minute resistance—which is a perfectly natural feature of her primal cognitive programming—she'll ask herself, "Do I know this guy?" and have a panorama of images of you in different settings to refer to.

With the rise of "in field" training on the Mystery model, the emphasis on esoteric techniques for controlling the behavior of women fell away. The new pickup artist was fun and positive. He had empathy with a woman's feminine needs, and was willing to remake himself into the kind of man able to fulfill those needs. Not the things she says she wants, or even the things she thinks she wants, in accordance with the cant espoused by our Rousseauist-egalitarian upbringing, but the primal needs designed into her neural circuitry forty thousand years ago, when people developed their social instincts while living, as Mystery puts it, "in a fifty-person society" with an alpha male at its head.

Evolutionary psychology and computer science, combined with behavioral economics's study of the systematic irrationality that is intrinsic to human cognition—that is to say, machine engineering combined with those growth areas in social scientific research that elaborate the materialistic, calculating, and hedonistic view of human nature that dominates "ideas" in the mainstream—all contributed to the pickup artist's vocabulary. "We backwards engineer the way the brain works, to figure out why she does what she does," says Mystery, who was living with his parents in Toronto and trying to make it as a magician while becoming known as the most eloquent of the message-board experts. According to Mystery, we are all "biological machines" programmed to do just two things: survive and replicate. And we go through life looking to align with people who will increase our likelihood to survive and replicate.

By offering a method and a pseudoscientific rhetoric to accompany it, the pickup artists offered hope to men who had lost hope. By giving students canned material to repeat, they overcame the single most intense social anxiety of any man in a club—that he will have nothing to say. By encouraging the men to see the activity of approaching women "as a video game," they provided emotional prophylaxis to men who were terrified of rejection. By assuming an authoritative role as paid experts, the lead pickup artists were able to tell men things they needed to hear: Lose the sweater. Shave your head. Get contacts. Get a tan. By introducing their students to the concept of subcommunication—body language, vocal intonation, and rhythm—they equipped them to begin the most important self-reappraisal they would ever do. The most valuable things the pickup artists told men were things that others had told them before, but that no one had ever directly linked to sex. Things like, for instance—"Smile." "Don't be the guy trying to look all serious and deep," the pickup artist Lovedrop told his students, with a wicked impression of a brooding face perched over a beer at a party. "Mr. Serious Deep Guy."

MYSTERY TAUGHT EIGHT MEN the rudiments of his art in the VH1 reality television series *The Pickup Artist*. It was a spectacle that managed to make Mystery's ruthlessly Darwinian method into the basis of heartwarming television. It was an exemplary product of our culture industries, on the cutting edge of the drive to combine uplift, self-help, and sociopathy into an appealing entertainment package.

The men were introduced—ordinary, slightly nerdy men—already "in field," failing to meet women at a bar. At the end of the night, they returned home without a single phone number in their pockets. Then Mystery appeared. "Who you are today," he said—slowly, clearly enunciating, maintaining eye contact with his audience, dramatically pausing—"dies here."

And we saw, right away, who his students were: a forty-three-year-old virgin, a fat guy, an Indian guy, an Asian guy, two computer nerds, and, a bit incongruously, a buff, good-looking Hispanic guy who was also a boxer. With the exception of this last, they were the sort of people who appear in the media only as comic figures. They remained so here—they could not sustain any other role—but there was no derision in the feelings they evoked; they were the protagonists on a quest for their manhood, and we watched them grow and change. They had been carefully vetted—they were awkward, they were abashed by their predicament, but not a single note of resentment toward women escaped them. One of the first rules that a pickup artist learns is that it's never her fault. "She's not a bitch," as Mystery put it. "She's just being a bitch to you." Because a beautiful woman, you see, has been hit on thousands of times in her life, and she has developed strategies for screening out the "bucketful of bore" that men want to impose on her. "Hi. My name's Charlie. What do you do?"

And thus the principle, "It's never her fault. It's always yours," reinforced the assumption that the game, properly played, could never fail. If at any point she shrugged you off, it was because you failed to do something essential in an earlier stage of seduction. This was, at one and the same time, a way of overcoming the ugly resentment that afflicts some AFCs, the ultimate form of self-protection, and, of course, a descent into total solipsism. Early on in the Game, after Strauss had his first "fool's mate" (the term for scoring with a woman just as eager as you to get laid on a given night, who does not require any game) and after he had "number-closed" a woman in a video store who turned out to be Dalene Kurtis, the Playmate of the Year (he's too frightened to call), he begins to notice it:

> It was then that I realized the downside to this whole venture. A gulf was opening between men and women in my mind. I was beginning to see women solely as measuring instruments to give me feedback on how I was progressing as a pickup artist. They were my crash-test dummies, identifiable only by hair colors and numbers—a blonde 7, a brunette 10. Even when I was having a deep conversation, learning a woman's dreams and point of view, in my mind I was just ticking off a box in my routine marked rapport. In bonding with men, I was developing an unhealthy attitude toward the opposite sex. And the most troubling thing about this new mind-set was that it seemed to be making me more successful with women.

**BUT THIS OBVIOUS OBJECTION** came later in the progression through the Game than any of the AFCs on the first few episodes of *The Pickup Artist* had yet reached. They had baby fat, they had smooth skin, they hadn't done a day of honest labor in their lives. They possessed that wide-eyed look—at once mentally slack, physically languid, and emotionally frightened—that you find when you meet those cosseted children of American suburbia who have remained mired in that shapeless setting. The Asian guy, when asked what sort of man he would like to be, responded, without missing a beat, "James Bond." The viewer cringed, a little, and squirmed, a little—a painful little ecstasy. Later on the fat guy, who managed to last until the later episodes, broke down in tears of appreciation, not just of his new skills, but of the new male friends he'd made. We learned that in real life he lived in his parents' basement, that there wasn't a door on his room. We learned that his only friends were friends he had made playing World of Warcraft. When, on a show that used his pain as a diversion from the emptiness of the lives of bored gawkers, whose diverted, emptied consciousness VH1 in turn sold to advertisers, he told his housemates that they were the coolest guys he had ever met, and the best friends he had ever known, with his face reddening and his eyes brimming over with tears, we knew that he meant it. This was good TV.

It was also a series-length infomercial. On the show, we watched pickup artistry slough off its vestiges of Ross Jeffries-style cynicism and pick up a new kind of cynicism: that of professional self-help. Mystery went from a dark seducer to a figure oozing that commercially factitious "caring" of our major corporations. These were some of the most helpless and emotionally immiserated men in America—and while it was true that Mystery had gotten rich off them, maybe he had done more for them than most therapists could. Admittedly, it was the two handsome guys who were there in the end, the handsome blond guy who made out with a stripper in the backseat of a limo, and the handsome and gregarious Hispanic guy who was ultimately selected by Mystery to complete his training as a master pickup artist. And, admittedly, the first guy off the show was the sweet Asian guy (as I predicted), and the second guy off the show was the forty-three-year-old virgin.

**THE PICKUP ARTISTS** were once good cinema because they were far outside the mainstream of American life and mores. The pickup artists became good television by embedding their practice within a familiar rhetoric of change and growth. In December 2007, Neil Strauss released a sequel, *Rules of the Game*—a slender guidebook in two sections that promised to help its readers "master the Game in thirty days." In fact, the book does not attempt to come close to delivering on that claim. A true PUA defines mastery according to Mystery's immortal formula: "five for five." That is—the true master has the skills to walk into a party, open five sets, and turn them into five girlfriends. The reader of *Rules of the Game* aims to get one date in thirty days. It is pitched at the most benighted of way-below-average frustrated chumps, consisting of bite-size assignments to complete each day (first assignment: say hello to a single stranger), interspersed with nuggets of wisdom fished from self-improvement books. The devious "neg" appears now as the more benign "disqualification." The wicked gleam in the eye of a man putting one over on the world has been carefully suppressed. A new earnestness brings the whole enterprise closer to the mainstream than it has ever been before.

The book's chastened tone makes this sequel feel like an act of expiation. "I didn't want to write this book," Strauss writes in the very first line. "I am as embarrassed to write this as you may be to pick it up." Strauss presents the book as his gift to the world. "Even though I had no such intentions when I wrote *The Game*, I started doing a few things in my spare time to help the many guys who reached out to me after its publications with emails, calls, and letters full of heart-wrenching stories. I coached frustrated teenagers, thirty-year-old virgins, recently divorced businessmen, even rock stars and billionaires." He observes that women have entire industries "to help cope with the challenges that come with being a woman in the world." He contrasts this to the cultural landscape of men. "Everywhere they turn, men are shown images of women they are supposed to desire. Yet there is little advice of substance available to help them learn to attract these women, to figure out who they are, to help them improve their lifestyle and social skills."

As pickup artistry became a business and changed the face it showed to the world, it lost the utopian, collaborative dimension of its earlier Internet days, when men produced knowledge together for free. Now Mystery competes for the dollars of men who pay up to $5,000 for a weekend spent in field. The website TheMysteryMethod.com is no longer affiliated with Mystery the man, who is suing and being sued by its current owners. Even while his show makes him the most visible face of the pickup-artist world, as Strauss is its best-known scribe, rivals and challengers in seduction lairs around the Internet announce technical breakthroughs in the science of pickup that claim to put Mystery's primitive techniques to shame.

**BUT WE SHOULD HAVE KNOWN** where it was heading all along. About two-thirds of the way into *The Game*, Strauss is dating ten women at once. "They were what PUAs call MLTRs— multiple long-term relationships. Unlike AFCs, I never lied to these girls. They all knew I was seeing other people. And, to my surprise, even if it didn't make all of them happy, none of them left me." Strauss had become what Freud called the primal father, though on the free-market model—he didn't mind if his women were having other relationships too, just as long as they responded when he called, and as long as he didn't owe them anything, by way of protection or otherwise, beyond offering enough value to keep them around in exchange for the value they offered him. It was a rational, realistic arrangement that everyone went into with eyes open, assented to voluntarily, was free to back out of at any time. Not backing out meant implicit consent, and implicit consent meant they remained because they calculated that they were better off by remaining. Everybody wins, right?

Early on, we watched as Strauss transformed himself into the man he has since become. He studied hypnotism, voice training, the Alexander Technique, and the secrets of a sexual shaman named Steve P., who gave him a method of stacking orgasms to make any woman squirt. Once he mastered the Game, this lovable loser who used to constantly find himself in LJBF ("Let's just be friends") Land could walk into every encounter in a bar with an HB (Hot Babe) *knowing* that he would be able to "kiss-close" her within half an hour.

By this time, Strauss was living with Mystery and a handful of other PUAs in Dean Martin's old mansion in the Hollywood Hills, a headquarters they named, in a reference to *Fight Club*, Project Hollywood. Men flew in from around the world to take classes with them. Soon Strauss would successfully run Game on Britney Spears. Courtney Love moved into the house. Strauss was about to stumble across a more or less foolproof technique for getting women to engage in a threesome.

And yet the whole endeavor had already begun its descent into hell. Strauss opens the book with a scene in which he drives a suicidal Mystery to a psychological clinic. Throughout the book, he builds a portrait of a profoundly damaged person with "a gaping hole in his soul." Mystery's goal in the Game was "a blonde 10 and an Asian 10, who will love each other as much as they love me." His goal in life was "for people to be envious of me, for women to want me and men to want to be me."

" 'You never got much love as a child, did you?' [Strauss] asked him.

" 'No,' he replied sheepishly."

They were living with two other pickup artists known by the handles Papa—a rich Asian boy—and Tyler Durden— the name of the new identity hallucinated into life by *Fight Club*'s psychotic narrator. Papa's immediate claim to fame was number-closing Paris Hilton at a taco stand (she never did come to a party at the mansion), but his obsession was building up the pickup-school business he was running with Tyler. Leading and profiting off men, rather than meeting women, becomes their dream. Tyler and Papa represented a new breed of pickup artist—preternaturally obsessed with observing and modeling the best PUAs, incapable of talking about anything else. These younger PUAs came to the Game before they developed autonomous personalities. They were nothing more than the sum of their programming.

Strauss began to see that the Game had turned many of these men into what he calls "social robots." He produced a long post for the online group discussion board called "Are You a Social Robot?"; the answer for most of them was clearly yes. And from there on out, Strauss started to tally up all the costs the PUAs had absorbed in exchange for their conquests, and the costs they imposed on others.

So while the first half of the book induces an irresistible high as we watch Strauss's brazen ascent, the second half of the book is a long, painful withdrawal from the inflated hopes placed on a handful of rather threadbare routines. Cruelty enters Strauss's behavior. Misogyny insinuates its way into the others'. They manipulate people and then despise them for their susceptibility.

Given an opportunity to fuck a coked-up porn star in a bathroom, Strauss can't get it up.

**THE GAME SAYS,** let whoever can attain transcendence attain it, whoever wants to pine for it, pine for it. As for us pickup artists, we serve the world as it is. We give it what it wants, and what it would ask for, if only it could bear the reality of its own desires.

The attitude of these men followed a sorrowful trajectory—from resentment toward women for their intractability to contempt for the same women upon their capitulation—though along the way, there were all the excitements that come with mastering a skill, as well as the incidental sexual gratification that one encounters in one's homosocial quest for self-empowerment. The men gleefully pursued an antinomian goal, and grew powerful because of their disregard for limits that other less desperate and disenchanted men still obeyed—the illusions that give love whatever meaning it still sustains in a world that has systematically converted every transcendent value into a mere advertising slogan, except for the one illusion whose sanctity we cannot yet extinguish, advertising slogan though it may be—that two souls might meet and assuage each other's loneliness.

The players of the Game made explicit the workings of a new sexual economy, one that was always implicit in the old, but was mediated by illusions that, it turns out, did more than merely obscure. We had disaggregated community, love, sex, and the family to allow a new protocol of maximum efficiency to establish itself. The Game players applied the logic of bourgeois productivity to slash open the myth of bourgeois romance. The mystery of romance yielded all its secrets to a method, ruthlessly deployed, which set its practitioners free from a fate that was never going to include them in its hoped-for happy endings anyway. Without explicitly criticizing it, they disclosed with unusual clarity the nature of the larger game we all play: one in which each player gives what he must and takes what he can. In this ordinary game, you judge your own value dispassionately, and cultivate the art of presenting it in the best light. Inasmuch as the purpose of the Game was to recalibrate a man's own programming to make him a better kind of biological machine, it was also a form of self-discovery, because every step along the way brought a new discovery of how much his own programming, and the world's, already consisted of self-maximizing behaviors that he simply hadn't mastered properly: You neither offer nor expect loyalty; in place of this premodern virtue, you offer honesty, transparency, and efficiency. If you find a better deal, you are free to go. If both members of a pair rationally calculate that they aren't likely to do better on the open marketplace than they are with each other, they commit, though they know that commitments are always reversible. They may search for stable foundations, but they should preserve flexibility for the day—its arrival is inevitable—when conditions change.

And so our individual quest to render ourselves invulnerable to the storms of fortune makes universal vulnerability the rule from which none of us can opt out. Inequality is built into the structure of this game, as nature assigns its endowments, and fortune doles out favorable circumstances in an unequal way. So the woman who does not have it all will not get it all: maybe she talks a little too loudly; maybe she weighs a little too much; and the man she wants will take what she offers without giving her what she seeks in return, and will not feel obliged to. So the man who has it all will get it all, and the man who has none will get none, and they all will be

grateful for the little they get, or grow sickened on the excess
of all they can have, or consume themselves with bitterness
knowing they are stuck with nothing, and be given commercial substitutes for what they cannot get on their own—
pornography that traffics in revenge fantasies, online dating
sites that reinforce the world's hierarchies.

The Game exposed that system by taking it apart piece
by piece and showing us how it worked. But it also shored it
up. It told us that through dogged effort and the application
of science, anyone could transform himself from pauper to
prince. Helena Rubinstein, the cosmetics magnate, once said
that there were no ugly women, only lazy ones. The promise
of magical self-transformation offered by the marketplace is
at the same time a pitiless injunction suggesting that women
born without the favor of beauty deserve the neglect they
experience from the opposite sex. And what good does our
pity do them anyway, if pity alone is all we are willing to give
to them? Better to give them the knowledge and techniques
they need to remake themselves as the world will have them.
Once informed, the responsibility for continued failure to rise
above genetic inheritance is theirs alone. So too, now, for the
men who didn't acquire Game.

Strauss's dark cautionary tale has a happy ending. The
contrast is as glaring as in one of those Hollywood endings
from the 1950s, the kind that spiteful directors would tack
on at the behest of the studios, deliberately playing up the
mechanical artifice to expose its falsity. In Strauss's case,
however, you feel that he is personally invested. He wants
to tell us that after extending his capability to such inhuman
lengths by such inhuman means, he's still human after all;

he's preserved that fragile part of himself that in the social robots has gone callous and cold. He wants us to know—and he wants himself to believe, you feel—that he's still capable of love. And so, he finally meets a woman who is impervious to the tactics of the Game. She is beautiful, she is smart, she is unflappable, and she can't be manipulated. "Lisa was neg-proof. Next to her, other girls seemed like incomplete human beings." And so on. She becomes his case of "one-itis"—and though he does go on the sex rampage that is the preferred PUA cure for the syndrome, he can't get her out of his mind. We are meant to diagnose this not as thwarted ego, or the Gamer Gamed, but as the stirrings of true love. When they finally fuck, he stays hard for four or five sessions in a row, and without the aid of Viagra. This must be the real thing.

At the end of the book, Strauss turns his back on the Game. It's a nice ending, but just because you leave the practice of the Game, you don't escape the world for which it is a useful guide. A year later, Wikipedia reports, Strauss's one true love left him for the British pop star Robbie Williams.

*n+1, 2008*

# PART IV

# 11

# WE OUT HERE

**A FEW YEARS BACK,** I wrote an article about Aaron Swartz, a hacker and activist who killed himself while under indictment for the unauthorized downloading of millions of academic-journal articles from an online archive. Swartz was devoted to an ethic of candid introspection, which he had practiced even at the age of seventeen, on a blog he kept as a freshman at Stanford University, in 2004. In September of that year, Swartz published a short post confessing to something that few take the time to consider. "However much I hate prejudice at a conscious level, I am nonetheless extremely prejudiced," he wrote:

> At my CS class, my eyes just passed over the large number of foreign and Asian students to land on mostly white ones (black ones too, occasionally). My Asian neighbor tried to make conversation with me and even though he had no accent, because of his face I imagined that he did. Had he been white, there is no question I would have started talking to him about stuff, but

instead I brushed him off. I begin to wonder how many people I've skipped over.

There's no term that quite captures what Swartz is describing here. He is admitting to an assumption that results in no act of visible hostility or hatred. He simply declines to extend to the Asian man who is seated next to him in class the same degree of friendliness and regard that he would extend to a white man. Perhaps Swartz's classmate asked himself later that day whether Swartz was merely a rude jerk, or whether there was a specifically racial component to what had happened. Maybe he didn't pause to wonder if the latter was the cause; maybe, as an Asian person living in the most Asian region of America, in a classroom full of others of his kind, at a school where Asians were strongly represented, he had no reason to think that anyone would treat him unkindly because of his race.

Or maybe the nameless Asian man came away from that incident inwardly torn, uncertain whether he had encountered subtle racism, his own social ineptitude, or the intrinsic hardness of the world. Maybe he suspected that all these things were factors—knowing all the while that to make an issue of it would seem an excessive response to an easily deniable claim about an event of small importance with many possible explanations.

If Swartz had thought more deeply about the reflexive aversion he felt toward the Asian man sitting next to him, he might have said something like this: "This person is likely to be a bore. This person is likely to be a grind. This person is likely to be lacking in emotional resonance, presence, humor, individuality, spontaneity, energy, imagination, and warmth. This person is likely to be passive, obedient, submissive, a hardworking nonentity, a nobody, a nullity, one of those mute lugubrious bespectacled glum-faced inscrutable spiky-haired presences haunting the library behind a stack of books, who gaze impassively into a column of figures or drool onto the table while napping in the wee hours." But it's doubtful he would have compiled that list. The whole point of living in a culture is that much of the labor of perception and judgment is done for you, spread through media, and absorbed through an imperceptible process that has no single author. Perhaps you, too, can envision being surrounded by Asian faces, all of them merging into one another in their meek self-effacement.

What we know for certain is that had he gotten to know Swartz, who would soon drop out of Stanford to help found the startup Reddit—that is to say, had Swartz not brushed him off because of his race—that nameless Asian man's life would have been changed for the better.

How do you quantify the effects of things that don't happen to you? I thought of this question when I glimpsed a picture of protesters at Yale University last fall, many of them black and female, bearing a sign with the following message:

WE OUT HERE<br>
WEVE BEEN HERE<br>
WE AINT LEAVING<br>
WE ARE LOVED

It was unclear to what extent the tension between insisting that you aren't leaving (presumably in defiance of someone or something that would prefer otherwise) and declaring that you are loved (presumably in solidarity with others who might doubt that this was true about themselves and others like them) was intentional. But the slogans testified to the sad but unmentioned fact that seemed to be at the core of these campus protests: that while you can prohibit the use of racial slurs through rules and norms, no administration or law can force someone to befriend you, or to love you, or to see you as a person who matters, or to notice you at all.

**I SHOULD CONFESS HERE** to the biases that influence my thinking. At the YMCA camp I attended when I was nine—the first (and, as it happens, the last) setting in which I was subjected to daily racial slurs—my father asked the counselors to ensure fair odds in the physical confrontations between me and the tormentors that he made clear were to be expected. It would not have occurred to him to demand that the administration protect me from bullies. Growing up meant forsaking the frightened victim in yourself, which had a way of sliding into disdain for the category of frightened victims in general.

I don't mean to suggest that I endured a tough upbringing or that my father was a hard man. My upbringing in a small New Jersey suburb was soft—especially when compared with the life, for instance, of my mother. The suffering she endured was squarely in the median range of what people born in Korea in the 1930s experienced. It was not unusual for American bombers to destroy your family's house during the Korean War. It was not unusual for your brother or father or sister to be killed by friendly fire. It was routine for proud

and ancient families like my mother's to be reduced to a des-
titute rabble living off the charity of American missionaries.
But her struggle did and does make most of the challenges
that you are likely to face as the child of Americans in a part
of the country where most of the kids assume they are headed
to college seem fantastically trivial in comparison.

The theory of microaggression can't help but seem to me
mostly an indicator of how radically devoid of other threats
our lives in America have become—at least in the fortunate
part of the country where people go to college. But maybe I've
grown habituated to conditions that today's young people feel
entitled to reject. And maybe I escaped the role of frightened
victim by finding others to victimize. When I think back to
those years when all my attitudes were formed, I think also of
the only black girl in the gifted-and-talented programs where
I first made friends. Her name was Shakina, and she was different in many respects from the suburban Jewish and Asian
male wiseasses who were the norm in those classes (if not in
the general population of their own schools). What an odious
term, "the gifted," to describe a group whose gifts mainly
consisted of being the children of lawyers and dentists and
professors and bankers—but let's not deny that there was a
certain facility we possessed or that it was a source of pride
to be segregated into a place where our need for instruction
tailored to our superior abilities would be honored. It should
not surprise anyone that being bullied during our school days
made us not lovers of humanity but victimizers of others the
moment we had the numbers on our side. And I guess it goes
without saying that we abused Shakina mercilessly, and that
even if our teachers had done more to forbid us from mocking

how she talked, as they sometimes tried to do, to little effect, no one could force us to see her as our equal.

In later years, in those same gifted classes, I encountered omnicompetent, hyperarticulate black teenagers who seemed on the fast track to world domination. They could code-switch from street vernacular to the smooth diction of the lecture hall, using each idiom to swell the power and persuasiveness of the other. They had forged in the crucible of their souls the resources necessary to survive and triumph in a world that wasn't inclined to believe in their existence until they had proved it. Everyone wanted to know them. Adversity, and the strength to meet it with forbearance and grace, had made them more interesting and complex than anyone who hadn't been exposed to the same stimulus that adversity ends up becoming for those who aren't destroyed by it. These people were cool.

They were also exceptional. The campus protests remind us that any system that requires exceptional fortitude from certain categories of people is an unjust one. The jargon that tried to name this injustice and serve as a tool in the struggle against it—white privilege, microaggression, safe space, etc.—caught on so fast because it named something that people recognized right away from their own lives. Like any new language that seeks to politicize everyday life, the terms were awkward, heavy-handed, and formulaic, but they gave confidence to people desiring redress for the subtle incursions on their dignity that they suspected were holding them back. The new vocabulary provided confirmation of what young people have always had reason to suspect—that the world was conspiring to strip them of their dignity and keep them in their place—and elevated those grievances to the status of a larger political project. Of course, the terms could easily become totalizing and portray the world as an "iron cage" in which crude identity categories determine everyone's fate in a way that is demonstrably false. In practice, the protesters wound up appealing to college bureaucrats to wipe away the accretions of the world's violent history.

And yet they also gave voice to an aspiration that people of my generation and older, who had grown up more isolated in a whiter America, had not thought could be expressed as a collective demand rather than as an individual wish: that all of us, even the unexceptional, could claim as a matter of right an equal share of existential comfort as those who had never had cause to think of themselves as the other. This still seems to me an impossible wish, and, like all impossible wishes, one that is charged with authoritarian potential. But those of us who have grown inured to life's quotidian brutalities—the ones we accept for ourselves and the ones we unthinkingly impose on others—should not be surprised that the young have a different sense of the possible than we do, or forget too readily what it was like before we were so inured.

*Harper's, 2016*

# IS IT OK TO BE WHITE?

**IS IT OK TO BE WHITE?** The question is at once disingenuous, facetious, satirical, and self-parodic. It is also one of the consequential questions being posed in earnest by the moral and political vanguards of our time. The question invites the typical reader to resist its implications—to deny that the question is one that anyone would think to ask, or that people are asking. But people have thought to ask it; they are asking it. It is the sort of question that one doesn't think to ask at all unless the answer is going to be no.

The pranksters who originally posed the question did so by interjecting a proposed answer into the physical world. The answer that they posted on signs and scraps of paper at universities and high schools in the United States and Canada was an affirmation in five uninflected words, rendered in a slender sans serif font in all caps on a plain white background: IT'S OK TO BE WHITE.

The flyers pose two questions: Who posted them? And why? The answer to the first question is an online network of ironic, postironic, and deadly earnest white nationalists, white supremacists, neo-Nazis, and others hosted on forums such as 4chan, the anonymous free-speech zone that is at once a predominant influence on the form that online communication now takes today and a cardinal exemplar of the social hazards of unfettered speech. The answer to the second question is deducible from the news coverage that the flyers received. The news media fulfilled the prank's aims, which were only achievable with its unwitting—and as the pranksters well understood, inevitable—collaboration.

"The news at 11 continues with a disturbing story from out of Montgomery County," began one newscast, noting that flyers were taped up at a local high school saying "It's OK to Be White." The monitor beside the anchor's face displayed the flyer reading "It's OK to Be White" alongside an all-caps graphic blaring "RACIST FLYERS?"

The contrast between the minatory framing and the innocuous message captured in that image was never going to shatter—as the delusional anonymous 4chan poster who conceived of the prank believed it would—the legitimacy of the media and deliver a "massive victory for the right in the culture war." Still, the campaign succeeded in generating gales of the malicious laughter, known as "lulz," that reverberate through this deplorable region of the Internet, as many of the reports the media dutifully generated resembled nothing so much as Christopher Guest mockumentaries brought to life. The campaign also showed that the meme brigade waging homemade mass psy-ops on the broader population of "normies" (referring to the ordinary Americans not yet inducted into the online culture wars) were evolving in their methods and learning from their adversaries in the competition to colonize minds and polarize the world into bitterly antagonistic factions.

"Black Lives Matter" was a simple declarative, instantly memorable, impossible to dispute, yet inviting dissent ("All Lives Matters") that would delegitimize the dissenters. "It's OK to Be White" reads like a non sequitur and induces people to pose questions without foisting conclusions on them. It invites dissenters to overreact. Whereas once the 4chan trolls gleefully trafficked in shock and provocation, they had now discovered the power of indirection and understatement, of confounding instead of confronting their enemies. Instructions for poster-makers sternly warned against altering the poster to include links to far-right websites, while leaders of the meme brigade on Twitter enjoined participants in the spread of hashtags to scrub their timelines of overt racism or sexism. These preparations indicated an awareness that their messaging had to be more moderate, which is a first step in any movement, in fact—becoming more moderate, and attracting mainstream support.

It is OK to be white. That some inner part of me flinches and hesitates to write the preceding sentences testifies to the bizarre, surreal, and yet all-too-salient polarization that has gripped the country since the election of Donald Trump. The statement is true—unambiguously so, and without qualification. One flinches to put oneself in agreement with a mob of white nationalists and white supremacists affirming that "It's OK to Be White"—but only long enough to recognize that dissenting from what is obviously true would serve the avowed interest of that same mob even more. One antiracist tweeter insisted that what the posters were really saying was "It's OK to be a white supremacist." But that's of course precisely what the posters didn't say. They also didn't say that it's a source of pride to be white, that being white makes you better than other people, or even that it's good to be white. It's just OK.

The cannier college administrations took care not to take the bait dangled in front of them by the posters, to reaffirm the diversity gospel while acknowledging the obvious truth. "There is and must be a place here for people of different ethnicities and skin colors, of different faith traditions or no faith traditions, of different nations, of different gender identities, of different political convictions," wrote one. "In that sense, it is indeed OK to be white—and to be black, to be brown, to be Christian, to be Muslim, to be straight, to be gay, to be conservative, to be liberal, and so on. We are stronger for this diversity of identities."

Part of responding to the coalition of white resentment from which the posters emerged in ways that stanches rather than feeds its growth, then, means taking stock of the way our own thinking has been affected by polarizing memes. In recent years, we've seen the rhetoric of social-justice activism change. Where once the targets of those concerned to fight injustice were "racism" and "sexism," today the targets are "whiteness" and "masculinity." In a characteristic passage, the *New Inquiry* writer Aaron Bady calls whiteness "an imaginary concept and a figment of the racist imagination." "Inextricable from racial subordination, whiteness has no other content at all," Bady writes. The newly pervasive coinage appears in writings explicitly focused on race, and in those that incidentally refer to it. A review of a book about millennials posted online by the journal *n+1* laments that "whiteness and masculinity continue to bedevil the socialist left, even in its committed anti-racist and feminist quarters," making explicit that it's not enough to be antiracist and feminist if you continue to remain, as the review's author, Gabriel Winant does, white and male.

The underlying premise is plain: that there is no whiteness independent of the domination of nonwhites, and no masculinity independent of the domination of women. Neither ever were, or ever can be, neutral descriptors of traits incidental to the person whom they characterize. They are instead forms of identity rooted in genocide, colonialism, and slavery that reproduce the violent conditions of their emergence everywhere they are treated as neutral descriptors of traits incidental to the person whom they characterize. They are what both permits and compels the white man to, as Bady puts it, "take his own experience as normal and privileged, and to presume all others to be debased copies of his own primary existence." A feminist writer at Public Books recently urged her readers to "attack masculinity directly. I don't mean that we should recuperate masculinity—that is, press men to identify with a kinder, gentler version of it—I mean that we should reject the idea that men have a psychic need to distinguish themselves from women in order to feel good about themselves." She later coined a neat apothegm that brings to completion certain latent tendencies in contemporary feminism: "The problem is not toxic masculinity; it's that masculinity is toxic."

In this new cosmology, there is no chastening, reforming, or accommodating retrograde modes of being that can leave the rest of the world safe from oppression, because these modes of being are radically and purely evil. They must be, in the parlance of the new antiracist activism, "abolished," "deconstructed," or "dismantled." For it is not racism but "whiteness" that is, as Ta-Nehisi Coates, the writer whose oracular pronouncements about an all-pervasive white supremacy emerged as a secular religion for liberals during the second term of America's first black president, put it in a recent essay on the Trump presidency, "an existential danger to the United States."

This rhetoric may appear at first to be primarily made up of bits of modish jargon drawn from certain academic subfields that have found new life on social media. And it is. But language has power, and a shift in usage has direct and intended consequences. The replacement of "racism" by "whiteness" as the problem that bedevils the world encodes another progressive meme within it: that because racism is "prejudice plus power," and all structural power is situated in the hands of whiteness, nonwhites may be capable of prejudice—a bad thing to be sure—but they cannot be racists. The default use of the term "whiteness" as the target of opprobrium bakes this contention into the language.

REPROGRAMMING LANGUAGE to achieve a political end is a strategy derived from poststructuralism, which holds that language is a system of difference in which the endless flux of signification is only arrested by the operation of power, and that this power is constitutive of a world (since our social world is constructed out of language) that will elevate some and enslave others, identifying some with truth, rationality, science, progress, justice, law, purpose, power, and agency; and others with emotion, grievance, superstition, particularism, benightedness, and submission: the former born to rule, the latter fit to be ruled. The shift corresponds to a broad turn away from liberal categories of thought and action, which emphasize laws and rights, to a Foucauldian account of a "malleable and insidious" racism, found in "the architecture of expectations, the ranking of authorities, the sway of circumstance, the nudge of defaults, and the grammar of culture. . . . It's in the norms, customs, precedents, and incentive structures of institutions, jobs, and roles."

Liberals think that there's a way to design a fair system of rules applicable to all people that would induce us to cease judging each other through the lens of the superficial physical traits that mark us as racially distinct. Poststructuralists think that the very idea of a fair system of rules applicable to all is a pernicious mystification disguising the partial interests of the dominant class as universality itself. No such universal position is possible; what remains to be done is the reengineering of norms, customs, and precedents to favor the marginalized.

This dense and rebarbative account of a racism that pervades the very structure of our shared reality remained largely sequestered in humanities departments until recently. Critics of such theories used to mock its pretensions to enact a form of political praxis in recondite journals. Now we know that the theorists were right—indeed they were more practical than their ostensibly more practically minded critics. But it took the invention of social media to realize the potential inherent in a deconstructive strategy to change the world.

Social media provided a medium for an iterative and collaborative process to turn critical race theory into sticky and contagious progressive memes. The memes were then injected directly into the collective progressive central nervous system. This applied deconstruction was made easy and fun through an automated, crowd-sourced process that resembles thought without involving any reasoning. As the game iterated, it achieved the power to shift the ground of permissible debate. A 2015 survey found that 40 percent of millennials believed that speech offensive to minorities should be prohibited.

Eventually, the new ways of thinking and talking begin to affect the form that activist campaigns and bureaucratic interventions in pursuit of diversity and inclusion take. By hopscotching from one meme to the next, certain ideas, such as the "progressive stack," which holds that one should deliberately call on marginalized people first, or ask white people to move to the back to make way for "racialized" people, become not just thinkable or defensible, but morally obligatory.

An instructor at the University of Pennsylvania became the target of right-wing outrage when she tweeted out a description of her classroom practice informed by the progressive stack. The university then announced that the instructor was acting in violation of its rules and that she would be disciplined. Her error in this was announcing aloud her adherence to the progressive stack.

Others who align themselves with the steadily advancing antiracist doxology will practice it without declaring it aloud. What begins as a provocation becomes a practice.

Anyone who objects to this as itself "racist" ("You're controlling people's access to resources simply on the basis of skin color! Isn't that the *definition* of racist?") simply proves that they don't grasp the underlying change in the intellectual terrain that has taken place. Such thinking remains embedded within the prior system of identity that was itself not just complicit with but, in fact, constitutive of racial domination. Those who resist any of the new account of racism are therefore themselves complicit with racism, and therefore racists. The white person who resists it exhibits "white fragility," itself a form of racism, all of which is inherent in and endemic to whiteness itself.

This intricate system of racial casuistry, worthy of Jesuits, is a beguiling compound of insight, partial truths, circular reasoning, and dogmatism operating within a self-enclosed system of reference immunized against critique and optimized for virality.

*Tablet, 2017*

## 13

# WHAT IS WHITE SUPREMACY?

**WHAT IS WHITE SUPREMACY?** An infographic distributed in 2005 by an antiracism nonprofit summarizes the myriad senses of this labile, capacious, and ever-expanding concept. The pyramid is divisible into socially acceptable and socially unacceptable forms of white supremacy. At the summit of the pyramid, above a dividing line, are the socially unacceptable forms of white supremacy—hate crimes, swastikas, the KKK, cross-burning, racial slurs, racist jokes, Nazis, and the N-word. Below the dividing line are the socially acceptable forms of white supremacy. These include "discriminatory lending"; "police murdering POC"; "Confederate flags"; "mass incarceration"; "school to prison pipeline"; "housing discrimination"; "anti-immigration policies/practices"; and "hiring discrimination."

The other entries on the list of "socially acceptable" white supremacy are worth listing in their entirety:

tokenism
bootstrap theory

cultural appropriation
white savior complex
blaming the victim
denial of racism
denial of white privilege
paternalism
racial profiling
assuming that intentions are good enough
racist mascots
not challenging racist jokes
self-appointed white ally
celebrating Columbus Day
color blindness
English-only initiatives
Eurocentric curriculum
believing we are "post-racial"
fearing people of color
"Don't blame me, I never owned slaves"
"But we're just one human family"
claiming reverse racism
not believing experiences of POC
virtuous victim narrative

There was a time in the not-so-distant past when the term "white supremacy" referred to slavery, genocide, colonialism, and segregation. This is still the definition that obtains for most of the general public. The taboo against white supremacy is grounded in a societal consensus rejecting those violent institutions and practices. A recent survey found that the percentage of Americans endorsing white supremacist views is in the single digits.

For the past few decades, academic departments in ethnic studies and critical race theory have elaborated a more expansive definition of white supremacy. Part of this account is historical, chronicling the ways that ostensibly race-neutral housing, educational, and criminal-justice policies worsened racial stratification in both intended and unintended ways. Part of it is theoretical, shifting away from a liberal individualist emphasis on laws and rights to a postmodern account of the ways that language and power embed relations of domination into the very structure of our shared reality. One academic refers to a "malleable and insidious" racism, found in "the architecture of expectations, the ranking of authorities, the sway of circumstance, the nudge of defaults, and the grammar of culture. . . . It's in the norms, customs, precedents, and incentive structures of institutions, jobs, and roles."

This "malleable and insidious" racism was more than malevolent people espousing hatred. It was implicit in things said and left unsaid. It hid away in the subconscious, exerting a subtle pressure on individual judgment and perception. This "structural" racism was manifest everywhere you looked and at every level of analysis. You could tease it out through a test like the IAT. You could find it written into criminal laws with racially disproportionate effects. You could interpret it in backhanded statements known as "microaggressions" that revealed hidden biases of the speaker. One example of a microaggression would be demanding to know where a person of

Asian descent is "really from" when they respond to your initial request by informing you that they are from the United States (which reveals that you regard Asian people as perpetual foreigners). Another would be telling an expensively dressed child of wealthy Nigerian immigrants who attended private boarding schools in Britain that "I don't really think of you as black" (revealing that your default expectation of black people is that they are not expensively dressed graduates of exclusive British boarding schools). These subtle indignities, trivial in themselves, could, when iterated over the span of a lifetime, reproduce patterns of stratification comparable to those under an overtly racist system—or so they theory went.

An all-pervading account of structural white supremacy makes the whole world into a field for both interpretation and contestation. Since the system of domination was unitary, attacking it at any point was to attack it everywhere. Since the system of domination was built into the language, campaigns on social media to alter usage were themselves a kind of political praxis. Social media has proven to be, among other things, a remarkably efficient means to inject novel ideas into a public sphere occupied by members of the media, activist, and intellectual classes, who use it, among other things, to coordinate an ever-advancing consensus about what being an antracist entails. There one can watch in real time as the unfolding of the internal logic of various ideological tendencies emerge, evolve, and reach their terminus. One handy rule of thumb is that any accusation or charge made as a half-ironic provocation in May will be avowed with earnest conviction in December and chanted by activists the following April. On October 4, for instance, a group of Black Lives Matter protesters disrupted a speech by a lawyer from the American Civil Liberties Union, chanting, among other slogans, "Liberalism Is White Supremacy," thus bringing to completion certain latent tendencies bubbling up on Twitter.

White supremacy encompassed differential expectations and outcomes both grave and trivial. It was why the cosmetics counter offered fewer options for those with darker-hued skin. It was why the heroes of Hollywood movies tended to be white men, why the Oscars were so white. It was why the CEOs and the leadership class were mostly white and male. It rested an invisible thumb on the scale of those who did nothing to seek it. It preserved the innocence of those whom it aided (white people) while denying those whom it fettered (everyone else) a readily articulable language to describe the obscure sources of their frustration. All those who were passive recipients of its favor were complicit with it. And complicity with white supremacy, like denial of white privilege, was itself a form of white supremacy.

There was both reward and risk involved with the promulgation of such a doctrine. There was catharsis in it. Everyone who had ever bridled at the easy assumption of the priority that certain white people carried with them recognized the descriptive value of the novel language immediately. It therefore spread through social media as rapidly as any novel jargon has ever spread. There was also power. The risk was inherent in the power: conceiving of daily life as a field of micropolitical contestation in which all are either privileged or oppressed conjured up the wish for remedial action, and because the enemy was everywhere and nowhere, the struggle to extirpate it would lack for a limiting principle.

"Microaggression" began its meteoric career as a therapeutic concept. It quickly became, in the hands of activists in virtual and real spaces, a weapon in an ideological war. A list of microaggressions circulated to professors at UC-Berkeley included statements such as "I think the most qualified person should get the job"; "America is a land of opportunity"; or "America is a melting pot." Each of these statements encodes a commonly held way of thinking about the country (that you could just make it here if you worked hard, that the best should rise to the top without favoring people based on their color, that newcomers should adapt to the manners and mores of the existing culture) that current generations of scholars now regard as pernicious—so pernicious that they no longer believe that they should be engaged with, debated, or debunked. They should instead be policed. As the pyramid of overt and covert white supremacy stipulates, "color-blindness" is itself a form of white supremacy. Two hundred thirty-one universities now have "bias response teams" that investigate the speech of professors and students, often with the aid of campus police officers, for infractions that include microaggressive speech.

What many of the beliefs now deemed microaggressive have in common is that they serve as conceptual and rhetorical obstacles to the spread of doctrines of group rights and compensatory justice that antiracist campaigners believed would be required to equalize the condition of black and white in America. The current definition of white supremacy is therefore best understood as an instrument in pursuit of a substantive political program. Policies such as thoroughgoing school and residential segregation, guaranteed employment, prison reform or abolition, and reparations for the coerced labor of slaves were considered and rejected in the wake of the civil rights movement. They have never been popular and are unlikely to win the assent of a country whose political tradition is one of limited government grounded in individual rights under law.

The troubling aspect of this campaign, in my view, is not the substantive politics that the antiracists wish to pursue. There is a body of critical and revisionist scholarship that makes a serious case for the necessity of exertions on behalf of historically disadvantaged minorities that exceed what a political doctrine of limited government and individual rights would be willing to contemplate. But the manner in which activists are seeking to win a debate is not through scholarship, persuasion, and debate. It's through the subornation of administrative and disciplinary power to delegitimize, stigmatize, disqualify, surveil, forbid, shame, and punish holders of contrary views.

"White supremacy" is the crux of this strategy, at once the source of its power and its ultimate vulnerability. For the term is both descriptive of an ever-expanding corpus of ideas and practices, and a weapon of opprobrium. It derives its power to anathematize from the consensus against the overt forms of white supremacy that appear above the dividing line. This power is contingent on the preservation of a narrow definition that sustains the consensus. The analogy with classification of state secrets obtains here: If everything is classified, as the saying goes, then nothing really is. When people cease to recognize the legitimacy of the classification regime, the state becomes far more leaky than it would be if you husbanded your power to classify more judiciously. Broadening the definition to encompass things that most people beyond a tiny coterie of activists consider to be benign can only inflate the value of the currency and water it down. Doing so while sustaining the power of term to surveil and punish those who are, by virtue of their skin color, presumptively complicit with it, might begin to feel like an act of aggression.

For while terms like "white supremacy" seem to have the power to trump any white liberal objection to them, and thus to give license to those who wield it—anyone curious as to what this can look like in practice, should find the online videos of the antiracist protests at Evergreen State College, wherein the president of that college asks his captors for permission to go to the bathroom and is instructed to hold it in— most of the country's white people are not liberal. The same poll that found that fewer than 10 percent of all respondents supported a white supremacist politics also found that 39 percent of all respondents agreed with the statement "white people are under attack in America."

Antiracists seized on this finding as further confirmation that tens of millions of Americans are white supremacists, thus renewing the charge that the country is a white supremacist country, thus surely increasing the number of white Americans who feel under attack. Actual white supremacists interpreted the findings as evidence of the potentially enormous size of the population receptive to their message, thus surely increasing the number of nonwhite Americans who fear the return of white supremacy. Now would be a good time to be careful with the meanings of words, aware of their multiple connotations, the uses to which they are being put, the ways they appear to different groups of people. If we can tweak our language and concepts to distinguish between great and petty instances of white supremacy, insisting on proportionality and nuance in our description of different kind of harms associated with race, it would go a long way to defuse some tension and ensure that the moral consensus that keeps the truly toxic isolated continues to hold. There are factions of awful people who benefit from this polarization. One of them occupies the White House.

*Tablet, 2017*

# ACKNOWLEDGMENTS

Thanks to all those who contributed in various ways to the pieces in this collection including but not limited to: my wife, Erika Kawalek Yang, Marco Roth, Chad Harbach, Keith Gessen, David Haskell, David Wallace-Wells, David Samuels, Willy Staley, Emily Cooke, Alexander Benaim, Joshua Pashman, Elif Batuman, Philip Fung, Jai-Hoon Yang, K. Hee Yang, Chinnie Ding, Isabel Howe, Matt Weiland, Remy Cawley, and Edward Orloff.